BORDERLESS

"These times demand poetry. They demand the diverse voices of women, placed front and centre where the oppressors can't avoid them, speaking the most powerful truths – their truths. At each turn, Borderless offers nothing but truth.

What better shows the inexhaustible strength and solidarity of women than having them speak together, in all of their diversity, their struggles and their joys?

Just as patriarchy is global, knowing no borders, so too must be our resistance. To read such fierce resistance page after page is to find strength in the moving words offered by this collection. This collection and the women within it are an inspiration."
— **SENATOR MEHREEN FARUQI**

"Women are finding their voices. We are flexing our vocal chords, our imaginations and our stories. Feeling their power, weighing their impact and turning up the volume. These poems, by women from a rich tapestry of backgrounds and experiences, are angry, moving and compelling. They will make you listen. They will help you understand." — **JANE CARO AM**

"We are experiencing a transformational moment and movement in our history for women.

We are witnessing seismic shifts in our societal and cultural attitudes towards women. But there remains a long way to go.

This is an important national and global conversation. However, it is critical that women from diverse backgrounds have their experiences reflected in that dialogue.

Women from culturally and linguistically diverse backgrounds; First Nations women; LGBTIQ women; women with disability – whose voices have been sidelined for too long – all have their own unique world views to share; their own unique marginalisation.

The inclusion of their stories ensures this is a changing moment and movement for all women. Their truths will be uncomfortable and provocative, but they must be heard with open hearts and open minds.

Borderless is a collection and an embodiment of these experiences."
— **THE HON. LINDA BURNEY MP**

"Borderless is the appropriate start of the title of this interesting mix of feminist transitional poetry. As a very early stateless refugee I am still reminded of the pain of patriarchal/patriotic exclusions that feminisms need to reject. So collecting and publishing this diverse collection reminds us of how we share diverse views!" — **EVA COX AO**

ACKNOWLEDGMENT OF COUNTRY

This book has been created on stolen land.
We would like to acknowledge the Ngunnawal, Ngarigo and Ngambri peoples, the traditional custodians of the land on which this book is published. We pay respect to their elders past, present and emerging, and we would like to extend that respect to all First Nations readers of this book.

BORDERLESS
A TRANSNATIONAL ANTHOLOGY OF FEMINIST POETRY

Edited by
SABA VASEFI
MELINDA SMITH
YVETTE HOLT

RECENT
WORK
PRESS

Borderless: A transnational anthology of feminist poetry
Recent Work Press
Canberra, Australia

Moral rights: each individual poet whose work appears in this anthology asserts their moral right to be identified as the author of their poem.

Copyright © in this collection Saba Vasefi. Copyright © for individual works remains with the authors.

Chief editor: Saba Vasefi
Editors: Melinda Smith, Yvette Holt
Consultant: Jane Messer
See p. 132 for acknowledgement of supporters of this volume.

ISBN: 978 0 64518 081 7 (paperback)

All rights reserved. This book is copyright. Except for private study, research, criticism or reviews as permitted under the Copyright Act, no part of this book may be reproduced, stored in a retrieval system, or transmitted in any form by any means without prior written permission. Enquiries should be addressed to the publisher.

Cover image: Wendy Sharpe, detail from "The woman that she was", oil on linen, 90x76cm, 2020. Reproduced with permission from the artist.

Cover design and layout: Caren Florance

recentworkpress.com

CONTENTS

Foreword   viii

Jordie Albiston *Name*	3
Ivy Alvarez *Binakbakán*	4
Cassandra Atherton *Single pink slipper*	5
Tusiata Avia *Elizabeth Pulman 1836–1900, photographer*	6
Maryam Azam *Routine Appointment*	8
Yasaman Bagheri *Drowned on Shore*	10
Bidisha *The Promise*	12
Merlinda Bobis *Lightly, Flower*	14
Candy Bowers *Protect bla(c)k women*	16
Jillian Boyd-Bowie *Matriarch*	17
Melinda Bufton FLOATING RIB PHANTASM SPECTACULAR (HIGH RELIEF)	18
Michelle Cahill *Taxidermy for Birds*	20
Vahni Capildeo READER, I TURN MEN INTO DEER	22
Anne Casey *Ingrain*	23
Bonny Cassidy *The race*	24
Claire G. Coleman *Momentum*	25
Emilie Collyer *Every day Antigone*	27
H I Cosar *I will*	29
Judith Nangala Crispin *Murder at Wave Hill*	30
Tricia Dearborn *Epoch*	32
Winnie Dunn *Bad Feminist: YouTube Edition*	33
Zoe Dzunko *Incedere*	34
Caren Florance *Predictive text fail*	36
Eugenia Flynn *My skin is on the ground*	37
Es Foong *My Words Through Your Ears*	38

Zenobia Frost	'all I want is a haircut that brings me peace'	40
Kween G	Hold the Light of Resistance	41
Mindy Gill	Garden After the Fall	43
Elena Gomez	Venus Blood	44
Charmaine Papertalk Green	Nyarlu Place Space Face	45
Eloise Grills	I love you so much I am ready to embrace queer death on screen	46
Susan Hawthorne	Bess and Surabhī	48
Sarah Holland-Batt	From the Manual of Southern Cassowary Husbandry	49
LK Holt	Category Error	51
Zeina Issa	The Midwife	52
Eleanor Jackson	Nominated intimacy	53
Lizzie Jarrett	#unapologeticallywoman	54
Jill Jones	These Deeds of a Woman	55
Gabrielle Journey Jones	Portable Lives	56
Jeanine Leane	On International Women's Day	57
Carissa Lee	tall poppy town	58
Kate Lilley	Wrongs of Woman (after Mary Wollstonecraft)	60
Bronwyn Lovell	Killer	61
Melissa Lucashenko	Screaming Blue Murder	63
Jennifer Maiden	Diary Poem: Uses Of Iron Ladies	64
Selina Tusitala Marsh	Mother's Machete	66
Jennifer Kemarre Martiniello	Being My Grandmothers (After Uluru)	68
So Mayer	Tally	70
Teena McCarthy	where have the Bush Marys gone?	71
Jazz Money	I don't sleep anymore	72
Lorna Munro	Snake skins	74
Dianty Ningrum	If I die	75

Maureen Jipyiliya Nampijinpa O'Keefe *What is a Feminist?*	76
Suneeta Peres da Costa *Roses*	78
Reneé Pettitt-Schipp *Southern Right Whale with Calf*	80
Anupama Pilbrow *Still Life of Flesh Wound Under Big Tree Poem*	81
Felicity Plunkett *Springturn*	82
Anne Poelina Wagaba *First Law: Matrix or Patrix*	84
Mel Ree *'3rd world mumma'*	86
Negar Rezvani *Silent Suffering*	89
Lynette Riley *I Am – birthed, born, directed, learnt, learned, strong & strengthened*	92
Samah Sabawi *Case # 70*	94
Sara M. Saleh *The (Not So) Secret Life of 3arab Girls: Our Raqs is Sharqi*	96
Kirli Saunders *Sacred Women Ways*	97
Kerri Shying *emotional laundress*	99
Beth Spencer *Dress me up*	103
Zainab Z Syed *A love like that*	104
Anne Walsh *The Wolves of Mayo*	106
Jen Webb *Refuse/refuge*	109
Ali Whitelock *LOOK AT HER*	110
Alison Whittaker *optimal*	111
Jessica L Wilkinson *Princess Fantasy, according to Jean Baudrillard*	114
Manal Younus *(untitled)*	116
Sista Zai Zanda *A Poem In Honour Of A Lioness Perfecting Her Balance Of Inner/Outer Power*	117
Contributor Biographies	121
Editor Biographies	131
Acknowledgements	132

FOREWORD

Welcome to *Borderless*. This unique anthology is the culmination of several years of effort. As such, I would like to tell you a little about where it has come from, and where it is going.

As someone who grew up under the censorship of the Islamic Republic of Iran, where any creative expression had to be passed through the filter of an authoritarian patriarchal regime, I believe imagination and creativity are forms of epistemic freedom, nonviolent action and civil resistance. For me, they have the capacity to combat a society's political domination and rescue its memory of diverse knowledge production. This is true not only for those living under the power matrix of a fundamentalist regime like the Islamic Republic of Iran, but also for those living in a society governed by the practices and legacies of European colonialism.

I arrived in Australia in 2010, and after years of dislocation managed to create a portable home in my state of exilic "in-betweenness" by studying the histories of women who were exiled before me. Their stories galvanised me to undertake my own work in the hope that I—in turn—might inspire women still struggling with internal or external exile.

From 2014 onward, I worked as Director of the Sydney International Women's Poetry and Arts Festival. The festival was an intellectual journey that propelled me beyond theory and toward practice. At the beginning of my work in this role, when I was searching for a venue for the event, I was advised by several human rights organisations to hold the festival in Western Sydney, which they considered to be the natural domicile of migrants.[1] This led me to consider whether the invisibility and marginalisation experienced by women of colour was related to them being compressed and boxed into particular spaces (such as the suburbs of Western Sydney), assigned to them by the dominant culture. I questioned these organisations' resistance to my decision to hold the festival elsewhere, and challenged their perception of the capabilities of an exiled woman by holding the event in the centre of the city at NSW Parliament House, effectively bringing subaltern voices from the margins to the centre.

---

[1] Many refugee communities settle in the suburbs of Western Sydney in New South Wales, Australia.

Many Australian community workers questioned my decision to hold the event in the centre of Sydney, not only because of the nature of my demand, but also because it was difficult for them to accept that a newly-arrived woman of colour was countering their assumption that they, as white Australians, should control the platform, while I, as a migrant, should capitulate to what they defined as suitable and appropriate for me and my community.

Despite this resistance, with the support of Senator Mehreen Faruqi I held the poetry festival in the city and at NSW Parliament House and it became a space of solidarity for diverse writers to platform their voices of persecution, and for audiences to appreciate their oppositional stance.

Through directing the festival, I gained greater exposure in my new society and met with feminist poets who wrote about systematic banishment in Western democracy and about their punished, marginalised bodies. Working with these liberationist women of colour committed to calling out the hegemonic conditions of segregation inspired me to initiate several other creative and academic projects—*Borderless*, this anthology, is one of them.

For someone like me who has been displaced and separated from her loved ones and family, creating a sense of unity has been a strategy for giving meaning to life and combating isolation. Distinct marginalised groups often gather separately, but it was my hope that Borderless might facilitate a platform for the alliance of diverse groups all standing together for cohesion.

Thus, my life experience and the exclusion I witnessed has motivated me to amplify other voices that yearn for unity. Just as I did with my Women's Poetry Festival, in the making of *Borderless* I was enthusiastic to partner with allies who believed in togetherness, unity and coalition. This time, however, we gathered not in the heart of Sydney, but at the heart of a book centred within a transnational feminist praxis. In doing so, I aimed to congregate the voices of First Nations, refugee and migrant women with the voices of Anglo Australians, as well as platform the voices of women from the LGBTQI and disability communities. I also wished to extend this diversity to the *Borderless* editorial team, so invited Melinda Smith and Yvette Henry Holt to bring their leadership skills, lived experience, cultural knowledge and expertise to the project. I thank them both wholeheartedly for their tireless work as co-editors.

After two years of work, *Borderless: A Transnational Anthology of Feminist Poetry* has finally emerged as a collection of poetics challenging mono-cultural norms and championing reterritorialisation through poetic imagination. This watershed, ground-breaking anthology brings together diverse, unique narratives for all readers to embrace and celebrate. By privileging women's experiences, the book allows the reader to interrogate historical invisibility and analyse the methods women use to challenge the concepts of sovereignty and monopoly, and combat the hard ideological lines that have historically erased women's agency and autonomy. The poems carry with them the ancestral journey of marginalised storytelling which has survived and thrived throughout the checkered seasons of colonialism and patriarchy, and together constitute a landmark collection of voices of substance.

Saba Vasefi

Editor-in-chief,
Borderless
Sydney, Australia
July 2021

POEMS

JORDIE ALBISTON
Name

It comes from the sire in a moment of
Errored desire   despite the good fight the
Rule resists & praxis transfigures it
Into immutable right   the womb is
A truth but the mother a myth & though

Half the earth is populus feminum
The birth of a girl is but property
Masculum & it just becomes fact that
Is that   o mater of mine   what art thine
Divine appellation   I seem to re-

Tain an account of your name in that part
Of my being taboo   & I thumb through
The temple the ledger of life   often
Get close to a mum or a wife but some-
How seem to miss any listing for *you*

IVY ALVAREZ
Binakbakán

How to Remove Stitches. Permanent Hair Removal. Everything You Need to Know about IUD Removal. Questions about Removal Companies. So often the body pays the price, the pressure exerted like arcana, a formula beyond my ken. Come back in two weeks and I'll take the stitches out, the nurse says to me, flinching at the gravel on my knee. I fell when that president was voted in, blood drying on my calf as I winced my way home. After decades on the pill, my hair was never as thick. I switched to the coil and it stayed there, a spiral in me, turning inward, its copper causing the death of millions, until I had it pulled free from me. I could not afford a removal company to move me, so I roped in my arms, a friend, and the one who let me go. My body hasn't let me sleep in months, not all the way through. I miss oblivion. The dreaming. I can't remember what I gave up. It must've been something.

Binakbakán: a Filipino idiom meaning someone who has been forced to give out a big amount (literally, one from whom something has been removed).

CASSANDRA ATHERTON

Single pink slipper   *For Zelda Sayre Fitzgerald*

One long exhalation into sleep. Heavy hips, fingertips, lips.

Everything that we have done is mine.

Her mind is a memory wheel: swimming by moonlight in Catcoma creek; breakfasts of champagne and fresh spinach; jumping into the fountain at Union Square. Scraps of journals, fragments of letters shining in another's prose like newly bobbed hair.

That is all my material.

Belladonna, potassium bromide, horse serum and morphine. Drawn-out rhythms of narrative and sleep. Darkness beats like a fast heart. 'Where's the fire?' This is not Westport. She'll die as another madwoman in the attic.

Trapped in sedation.

Lost in silence.

None of it is yours.

Italicised lines taken from F. Scott Fitzgerald, Typescript, May 28, 1933.

TUSIATA AVIA
Elizabeth Pulman 1836–1900, photographer

When Lindauer did his paintings
of all those rangatira
I believe, Elizabeth, he took some of your photos
without permission, after you were dead
he projected them up onto his canvasses and traced around
the lines. And then it was just a matter of colouring in.

The people from the museum tell me
that the rangatira came to you:
Ta Whiao, Maori King
Te Tupa Ra Ma, Maori Queen
Monga Rewi, Maniapoto tribe, Waikato
Maia Tuture
Tiki Tiki and her pepi
Keate and Peea in a hongi
Marau Kingi
Te Retimana, Terapoutu
Wiremu and Rangitoia in a hongi
Anehana
This is how you wrote them down.

The people from the museum tell me the rangatira came to you
they commissioned you to photograph them
dozens of copies at a time, small as calling cards.
And for the King and Queen and rangatira, the largest prints
commensurate with their status.

The finest moko
the rangatira's cloak
the patu
the feathers, the pounamu
the taiaha
the face looking off into the distance.
As you count down the seconds to exposure, Elizabeth
you manage somehow to stop the wriggling baby blurring.

Photos like these have always made me squirm
their likeness to my own ancestors, bare-breasted in ceremonial headdress
arranged in some studio in Apia somewhere.
I don't know how those ethnographic portraits came about
but I know how they've made me feel all these years.

So, Elizabeth, to learn that yours were commissioned
that you were in their employ, makes me feel relief
and respect for you. After all, who could make King Ta Whiao sit?

The people from the museum also tell me that you were a
        good photographer
I can see that, Elizabeth. But no one knows your name now,
        unlike Lindauer's
and no one took any notice of your copyright copperplated carefully
on the bottom of every one of those photos.

Photos from: Pulman album: ID: PH- 2015-10/.
Contributor Elizabeth Pulman, War Memorial
Museum, Auckland, New Zealand

rangatira: person of high rank
moko kauae: traditional Maori facial tattoo
rangatira's cloak: korowai
patu: club/ hand weapon
pounamu: New Zealand weapon
taiaha: spear like weapon

MARYAM AZAM
Routine Appointment

Two women stop me at the entrance.
Do you have any symptoms?
Up until this point I had no symptoms
but just like that my nose starts to run
I suck it up and tell them I don't while
the baby rolls inside, all over my nerves
Have you been to one of the hotspot areas?
One of them lifts her temp gun to my head,
confirms I'm not running a fever, then
hands me a surgical mask and purple wristband

The man at the front of the line
to the Women's Health Clinic
can't join his wife for her appointment.
He says she can't speak English
and he needs to translate for her –
that's a hard no – he says can you have
me on a video call to translate –
again no, but there's a translator service
and for $97 a translator can attend
but this needs to be arranged in advance –

I want to sniff again and the baby kicks hard
so I focus on holding up my heavy,
drooping body with a hand on my hip.
I read and re-read the two posters on the wall:
Sleep on your side when baby's inside
List of Covid hotspots
The man stalks past me; his wife has gone into the clinic.
Despite the wristband, I'm questioned about Covid again.
The midwife says, find a seat somewhere, the doctor will call –

The six seats outside the clinic are taken
so I sit on a hard mosaic bench in the main foyer.
I read and re-read *your baby at 32 weeks*
until a private number calls. It's the doctor.
She explains that the phone consultation

is one of their Covid measures. Is baby moving well?
Am I feeling well? There's not much more to say.
Then she says, meet me outside the clinic, I'll bring
you inside to check baby's heartbeat – we're meeting
face to face? – It's part of the routine –
I hobble back.

YASAMAN BAGHERI

Drowned on Shore   translated by Saba Vasefi

Reborn from the water,
I am undrowned.

It rains between the children's eyebrows
and with every drop their floating corpses
sink deeper into the sea.

Among the myriad corpses
I survived
to remember
their displaced faces.

Her eyes were blue
like a drop from the Pacific Ocean.
It was as if she was shouting
I was here!
a five year old girl,
red nail polish
on her little fingers
firmly attached to the boat rope.

The mothers and fathers,
one hand raised to pray,
the other on their children's shoulders.

The wave was a dreadful death
rolling towards us;
towards us, whose shore was not our home.

Either the generous sea
embraced us—the banished—
and we could die from suffocation
or perish later from withdrawal syndrome
in a mouldy tent.

غرق شده در خشکی
یاسمن باقری

دوباره متولد شده از آب،
من غرق نشده.

باران میان دو ابروی کودکان می بارید
و با هر قطره
جسدهای شناورشان
عمیق تر در اقیانوس پایین می رفـ.

میان صدها جنازه
من زنده ماندم
تا صورت های ویلانشان را به یاد بیاورم

چشمانش مثل دو قطره از اقیانوس آرام، آبی بود
انگار داد می زد
که روزی در این جا بوده است
دختر پنج ساله
لاک قرمز
و انگشتان کوچکش
که طناب قایق را محکم چسبیده بود.

مادرها و پدرها
یک دست به دعا، بالا
دست دیگر روی شانه کودکانشان

موج مثل مرگی مهیب
به سمت ما می آمد
به سمت ما
که ساحل خانه مان نبود.

دریا سخاوتمندتر ما رانده شده ها را
در آغوش می گرفت
و ما فقط می توانستیم بمیریم
با خفگی
یا بعدتر تلف شویم
از سندرم استعفا
در چادرهای کپک زده نارو.

BIDISHA

The Promise

Every December I renew the curse. I go to the end of the garden at night
And map out a semicircle of dripping black candles on the low stone wall.
With a fistful of nails I pierce my perpetrator's photograph through the eyes
And repeat the words of the verse I've written down. Then I burn the paper.
The ashes, wax and embers mark the wall and I let nature take care of them.
I fantasise about meeting my perpetrator alone in Central London in
          winter time
And saying to him what I've wanted to say for eleven years now.
          'I do not forgive
And I'll never forget. You are an abusive man and you will pay for
          what you did.
Justice must be done, by law or by karma. I will see you in prison, or
          in the grave.'
I keep whispering the words until they run together in a long continuous
          hiss
And I know that he can hear them and that deep in his nightmares,
          he trembles.
First he killed me and now I'm going to kill him, that's the deal, and so
          he waits.
My rage is my secret weapon and my dearest friend. It keeps me young.
Anger is my first response to anything and it gives me endless energy.
My rage enables me to work out for hours every day, like an athlete.
I love my anger more than love and friendship and tenderness and joy.
I don't want to be happy, I want to express my rage and my pain.
I don't want to move on, I want revenge and I'll get it.
I am capable of anything and I'll happily go to prison for it.
The singed smell stains my fingertips and the smoke makes my eyes smart.
The trees at the edge of the garden rustle around me. This is my family home.
I've lived here all my life and when I'm away from it I feel small and
          vulnerable.
After setting my curse for the next year I feel bathed in cool clear night light.
I go back inside and drink a mug of lovely hot milk on the sofa to warm up.
I go into town the next day and am certain I'll bump into him, but I never do.

When I travel on the Tube I look at them and think about how much I hate them.
They make my skin crawl and dwelling on this makes me feel strong and satisfied.
I want to tell them that as much as they hate us, the feeling is totally mutual.
They say that before you get revenge you must first dig two graves
I am happy to do so until my muscles hurt and dirt cakes my nails.
I pretend to read my book and lift my fingertips to my face. They still smell singed.
I know I need to renew my promise for another year when the burning smell fades.

MERLINDA BOBIS

Lightly, Flower

> For all Warrior Women:
> on seeing 'The Dance of Peace'
> (Riga, Latvia)

Lightly, flower, rest
on the curve of her shoulder

where her lover's brow rested
before returning to the trenches,
where her daughter hid
her fear of the uniforms,
where her son breathed
his last after a stray bullet.

Lightly, flower, rest
as you did on the curve of a hill

before its trenches
or the fear, the bullets
blind, so how could they tell
the daughter from the uniform,
the son from the soldier
on a warm summer day?

Lightly, flower, rest
as you did on the curve of her cheek

on a long ago summer
when she rested on the hill
with her lover—how heady
those lilies of the valley
and the kiss warmer,
fuller than summer.

Lightly, flower, rest
on the curve of her shoulder

where a rifle rested
when she took to the hill
sans lover daughter son
hearth home lost
to the war—how heavy
the wish to be free.

Lightly, flower, rest
on the curve of the hill

where she fell.
Lightly, gently, please
on the curve gone deeper
from all the resting without rest,
even now, never still
like the earth.

'Lightly, Flower' was inspired by seeing flowers resting on the shoulders of one of the dancers in the sculpture 'The Dance of Peace' by Parsla Zalkalne in Riga, Latvia, and the nearby memorials for all those shot in the city on 20 January 1991 during The Barricades against the Soviets. The sculpture itself bears bullet marks from Soviet machine guns when they attacked the Latvian Ministry of the Interior. This poem travels beyond Latvia to all other places and peoples (including women who have taken up arms) that have fought for independence against colonising forces through history until the present time. This poem is for all women warriors who will never rest! For many of them, the shooting has not ended. So lightly, gently, please, stray flowers.

CANDY BOWERS
Protect bla(c)k women

Protect bla(c)k women
Reciprocity is well over due
Protect bla(c)k women
Bone, blood, flesh and sinew
Protect bla(c)k women
Caretakers of ancient truths
Protect bla(c)k women
Makers of rain and stew
Protect bla(c)k women
Strong, sweet and true
Protect bla(c)k women
Silver, green, magenta and blue
Protect bla(c)k women
Seen and see-through
Protect bla(c)k women
We have new futures to pursue

JILLIAN BOYD-BOWIE
Matriarch

Soft grey skies, occupied poignant cries
of misplaced empresses in days gone by.

Revered powers burnt upon the woods over time, robbed
by men with shaky hands and rickety legs starved in status
building disempowering systemic structures
to bury our shine.

To live beneath, and not by.

Woman come, sit with me upon our matrilineal throne
blameless bare bosoms mothering
souls stripped bare, uncovering spoils.

Deep calls unto deep lines through birdsongs
of ancient oracles.

Time travellers falling like rain from soft grey clouds
saturating sacred spaces of woman's business
sifting into warm hands of healers.

Knowledge holders outpouring
into the cusps of protectors
nurturing the famished into bellies full
and crowded minds.

Delivering newfound life into scriptures of old.

Drink your portion of historical nobility
a stolid state you dare not be.
To your role pledge fidelity.
Rest in your inheritance duly.
Welcome to your country.

MELINDA BUFTON
FLOATING RIB PHANTASM SPECTACULAR (HIGH RELIEF)

I resist the urge to climb right in
to the melted wax of the stubby gift candle and confit
myself. Superannuated duck with
aaaaall my soft fillets taken care of.
Or potted like a treat for a later time.
This morning the barista said
I work in the kitchen some days and we all agree
back there
that when you've put new oil in the fryer the surface is so
glistening and clean you just really want to
     put your hand right in it.
We all do. We all just want to.

Wax melts combine your scented atmospherics in a
safer form. It isn't what you think it is;
they are boneless candles. Without ribs, and I imagine
a poem that is ONLY RIBS. For fortitude and crafty display.
Or, just for showing off. This instagrammeur is carefully moving towards
WAX MELTS as a sideline. To herself, in her main account, where it is just
     beautiful fleshy
shots where she dares you to look. When the wax melts are done you can feel
     melancholy
but also RELIEVED that they are so careful and there is never a wick.
Spineless good times.
Max welts.

The poem that is only ribs, wicks, welts and confit

Ah there you are my darling. I have taken my own ribs and adopted them out for some other venture. Starting from scratch you create the voodoo dolly of your wildest dreams, only this one is your
own good self. Keep the leather in, make the fluff to the outside. Peachy face skin and peachy peach skin. This is way beyond self portrait but all the way to rib tickler. NOW I HAVE EMERGED FROM THE MELTED TUB OF WAXX I AM KNOWN BY THE IMPRESSION I LEAVE BEHIND AND IF U R CURIOUS
AS MANY ARE
YOU CAN RE-CREATE ME ANY TIME AS A WAX OR ART PROJECT BY CASTING A BRONZE
or a copper, my clover all over

MICHELLE CAHILL

Taxidermy for Birds

'It is our mothers, wives, daughters, sisters, friends, neighbours, and co-workers who are being victimized.'   *—Kimberelé Crenshaw*

my scars are invisible, loose threads
the neck snipped, eyes removed
entrails, barren as an open cut megamine,
a bird quarantined, a fugitive
routinely flying into glass, each sudden death

there's no ledger for this
        incremental abuse, its method acting

in my sleeve are three hand-made cards,
decorated with inky, delicate rosebuds,
signed by missing person (nb ages 13 – 16)
a house surrounded by trees on a battle-axe
hidden from Google Maps   a therapy couch,
and a classroom became complicit
        the barrister advises that partial
      vanishing is best served by restraint, surveillance
possibly, & promises to write a letter
but not today

outside, the sun's blazing, a missed call might be
        B.T. or Bitcoin
at Southern Cross Station, it floods my mind
insistently – the video of a Muslim man beating his wife,
after being thrashed for carrying beef,
(so she's a victim of husband and Hindu mob)

the photographs breathe light under bevelled glass

i listen to the silent, psychic leaves, the sting
of hands felt cold touching the face,   faintly, i try
to remember the exact moment courage fails,
        daring to be free
    always this way,
when violence rifles a woman's body

        take a sprinkle of borax, cornstarch,
        do not cut the feathers
    stuff with broken time, blunt tongue,
    a dash of impudence   cold as bone, facts, facts,
        feathering, kept dry,
    a ribbon of life   shimmering, sewn,
        seemingly neutral words spike
    fixed to wings that are wired
    into the serial mount

VAHNI CAPILDEO
READER, I TURN MEN INTO DEER

Told me about a childhood. Running free through rain-
forest. Those were the best days! On all those paths, he
never saw a snake... Told him about a childhood
within walls, snake in the postbox, snakelet unearthed
wriggling, never-seen snake of the drain moving
heavy stones we put to block its resting place. Yard
had the displaced inhabitants of forest... He
would've been running through with his gun and smoke-bright eyes.
Decades and decayeds. *What you see, what you do, what*
you say, what you know, what you believe, what you have
been storying, your self in storage, your storied
self. Decayeds and decades. Is dangerous. Forest
becomes forensics. The frond is dissected. Oh,
it waves over all those paths. Equivocations.
You see? You do? To me? As if I am a wo-
man? Come on. He says. To control. Coming on. He
knows... *Control. You believe. The narrative. What thorns*
mistaken for companions. What canopy. What
shutting out. He discs his eyes. His hooves hurt.

ANNE CASEY

Ingrain

With a practised twist, the man on tv
is prising open the fragile mouth,
probing tender flesh unable to resist,
orbs of sunlight string glistening water behind.
Inside the injured tissue, he leaves a small stone—
in time, it will grow a pearly cyst
to smooth over the rough intrusion.

In the jumble of a city flea market once,
I couldn't resist
a string of aged pearls, their soft peach glow
alluring from velvet folds—
I realise now why
no matter how I would twist them,
they would find a way to choke.

How a man's hand can close
over a small mouth, encircle a throat—
unable to resist, injured tissue accepts the stone.
I almost drowned once, refound how words
won't form in the absence of air.
If I could form the words now,
I would tell you how you can drown on dry land.

Never take me to an oyster farm—
all those closed mouths
not forming words under water,
slowly growing over their small stones.
There are places where a woman can be stoned for failing
to resist a man, her pulped flesh left
to ripen around the stones.

BONNY CASSIDY
The race

We wonder what we're gonna hit us fathers of two tin lids us fence installers. Pale warmed and enticed to pit ourselves against a poorly lit dive a bit competitive we are. Focused on the names of the future channeling the break-up. And taking off us all these things we flat out race through the exhibit after the siren into dark. Left alone to be loose unheard of. So where the hell do we go running harder. She doesn't look right our mother we don't hear her signals we're too ahead. Fed up like a little town mopping its heavy duty wishes. Our family and food and time skips without natural rhythm the flag we first knew her eye shadow blazing. We will sue generation to generation snaking in to spoil tradition. In numbers in waves on street corners in shopping fall out not jump backseat. Bristling truckloads face down the path after the finishing that history just about everybody understood.

CLAIRE G. COLEMAN

Momentum

      I

Patria
The Nation is a father
Matrix
The land is a woman/mother
And I can't help but feel

The colony,
The fatherland imposed over the mother
Is an abusive marriage/marital rape

Decolonise, crawl out from under,
Get off your back and stand; stand up
And here the nation stands, victim blaming;
When we blakfulla have the audacity to say
No means no. Stand; stand up – strong
And fight and perhaps
That's what decolonisation is
No means no.

      II

Pro Patria Mori

Hate is rising; Fake patriots
They think freedom is slavery
Believe the Old Lie. They will
Die for the fatherland while they
Hasten mother Earth to her death.

And Christofascists destroy the mother
In the name of the big beard father in the sky
Forgetting in the end it will be their children
Without God's Green Earth to live upon

I have no children but I care more than they do.

III

I remember "reclaim the night"
We fought to make the streets safe
Women, united against violence
Against; that the streets were not ours

I remember "no means no"
I remember pro choice
I remember autonomy
I remember agency

We should not have to fight for
Our right to live; blak women
Have never been given a choice

Remember in a generation
This was our chance, our moment/momentum, perhaps our last
We could have fought shoulder to shoulder
Even if we lost; we will remember
This moment

EMILIE COLLYER

Every day Antigone

Antigone is in every kitchen
        ordinary daylight bravery
autumn leaf suburbs
        and brutalist housing towers

she's wearing new pink kicks
        dragging on a cotton-pilled sweater
mundane domestic the room
        with knives an oven

a sunken silver hole shaped
        like a cradle
echoes of all the kitchens
        that came before

dad's done something rotten
        a sister in another room
who's neither violent nor erotic
        surviving her own unhappiness

on this ordinary day all the
        Antigones stand up in their
dry mouth way against a slapstick
        joke a sweaty hand a gun held

by an invisible man they each
        stand with grumbling stomachs
coffee breath toast crumbs
        in their toothbrushes

they open their mouths
        these everyday Antigones

        rise   [felled]
        speak   [silenced]

    and nobody makes a big deal
        of what happens
    her body not meat enough
        to feed the news cycle machine

        maybe a heartsick
    mother or friend who wonders
        at the end of the day
    why the kitchen is so empty

        dishes silent lights on
    waiting for every Antigone
        to get home safe
    for all of her stories to be told

H I COSAR
I will

I will get off my throne
heaping goddess wings
powers, strengths, strings
on velvety seats
I am no one's goddess

I will take off heavy robes
free my lions and bulls
I will break the gate
and scatter the jewels
(except lapis lazuli)
there will be no sign of what was

I will jump and fall
because I want real
I will crawl through womb
again, to being woman

I will be insatiable
I will not learn from mistakes
I will face results
of terrible decisions

I will be wild and free
no roofs no rings
no names on paper
I will know who I am

I will have my breath
unyielding obstinance
clouds and earth
I will create havoc
I will want and want
until the end
to make up for all we lost

JUDITH NANGALA CRISPIN
Murder at Wave Hill

i:

Yes, he is beautiful, the boy dancing with men, *purlapa*, snake story— his skin gleams oil and iron-red ochre, she watches his musculature, his torso lithe as a red-belly black.

In Wave Hill, population 334, there are no secrets.

She plays cards with old ladies in the road, for welfare money, for cigarettes and grog. He calls her to the window of his Holden V8. She is a love spell, the word 'Deadly' in sequins across her chest, eyelids painted Beyoncé blue. Night,

already fallen to dust and insect wings, the hanging planets, spindrift stellar fields over the houses. She sees auras, she tells him, not like *ngangkari*— like a faith healer, like someone holy, someone from outer space.

He gives her a motel Bible, from a room at Top Springs, shows her antique playing cards online, with pictures of doves and owls, peacocks. He drives to Katherine to buy her a Woolworths chicken.

ii:

When the baby comes they move into a sheet metal donga, coloured fairylights along the back fence. She dreams of a honeymoon at Top Springs, of white towels folded into swans.

When the baby comes, he tells her he might take up rugby.

In a smoke-filled room, she changes the baby, turns up her bluetooth speaker— rap music pouring into their yard of noisy dogs, the scorpion-filled weeds beneath the car with its windscreen shot out, that night he came home too drunk to aim a rifle.

They fight. They tip over the sofa looking for change, and one day, the word 'suicide' creeps into the donga like a huntsman.

She stops taking the medication, watches crows with renewed interest.

He joins the rugby team. While he's at training, she takes kitchen scissors into the yard, opening and closing them like a beak.

They survive Christmas.

iii:

Now, in January, he sees the bare shoulders of another girl— the falling strap of her dress is a road to a different life.

Somewhere, on a night of bottles, far beyond the town lights' reach, they lie on their backs tracking comets, star formations— the skyworld of animals. Hammered silver, the Milky Way spins asteroids and cosmic dust,

spacejunk, the exploded ruins of stars— all the night's dark until trees resume their daylight forms and parrots read their canticles to the sun.

And now he sees how things end.

The boy moves his things out of the donga, mumbling excuses— we fight too much. This one right skin, prettier. The words 'child support' drop in the space between them, cold as the light of outer planets.

In the kitchen, in her tiredness, she feeds the baby— her brain burning, sees crows perched in a corner of the room, houselights turning on in the street, and in those houses, other girls at their mirrors, putting on lipstick, wiping it off.

She sleeps alone, motel bible beneath her pillow.

iv:

In a town like Wave Hill, there are no secrets.

Yes, the young mother is beautiful. She helps him support the new baby's neck, keep its tiny head from falling. He tells her his ex-wife is crazy— gone beyond some unknown vanishing point, even pulled out her eyelashes.

The ex-wife watches them together at the park, at the swimming pool— sees them smirking behind supermarket shelves, glancing back at her from the checkout and laughing. She returns nappies and baby formula to the shelf.

She buys a steel claw hammer.
She buys a knife.

TRICIA DEARBORN
Epoch   *For Ngaire*

It will bloom once more before it's gone, small potent organ,
shaped (I read) like an upside-down pear —
shed its lining one more time before the hormones' call
falls only on deaf tissues. The organs that surround it now
will settle to their slightly altered places in the pelvis. The bladder
will take back its space, freed from uterine protrusion. No more for you
the wringing pain, the compulsory horizontal, the hassle
of the unmistakeable feeling and the tamponless handbag.
Though other sloughings may be needed — more sweat, more tears,
more manuscripts. The ovaries will still dictate the body's
oceanic swell and fall, the tides will just be different.

WINNIE DUNN

Bad Feminist: YouTube Edition

Notifications:
Acne. Skin of colour. Hyperpigmentation. White cast.
UV rays. Retinol. Anti-age. Tighten. Saggy skin. Detox?

Tasks. Team meeting. Eliminated. Elect to skip vote. Emergency.
Admin. Report. Use. Sabotage. EVERYBODY GETTING BODIED!

Today's video. Sponsored by Athletic Greens. Nutritional insurance.
Sugar ruins. I'm vegan so I'm. Greens, greens, greens. Healthy = happy.

Up next:
- Can he guess which one is breastmilk blindfolded?
- 73 Questions with Ariana Grande | Vogue
- *NEW* GLASS SKIN CARE ROUTINE & Glass Skin Makeup
- A Ballerina's Entire Day from Waking Up to Showtime
- 15 Minute Arm Burnout (weightless upper body workout)
- Answering UNGODLY & JUICY girl talk questions
- Reacting to Weird Hentai Because You Wanted This
- Eight ways to stay looking young for life

Recommended for you:
Return to the Land: A Tongan woman's journey to finding peace and purpose.

ZOE DZUNKO

Incedere

Morning of wet glass, skyless vistas. Her stomach falls back in, a window slamming shut. Another expired epoch. I am momentarily amnesic my damp brain and its moving clouds: a slick, a saccade, a flash of shifting light. She is in the room with me now. My life reel. Could I remember this or have I superimposed the firmament of her face with the mobile's dangling objects? She is welcoming me to the new world. A curl brushed behind the ear. Down the hall, a hairdryer cooks the webbed growth of dead days. The first news of the morning spirals in with its bad stories: faulty wiring has arrived to cinder another timber home, the family dreaming through overcast oblivion, their flesh tones dimming. The door is kicked into a splinter but everything has already happened. It is useless cursing this muffled mouth of mine, but what I lack in my language is a way of asking for what I need: something like a hormone with its broken logic, ancient mind refusing to submit to the details. My body is worth the weight of air my life is a mute testimony. Perhaps she knows it, or maybe she is learning that when miracles arrive, they come stitched to a series of unfortunate circumstances to circumvent. A fresh fear with its margin of tidy slices. Before they put her under does she locate a reservoir she would not recall begging for? I would ask her how but I'm on my back again. My arms slipping their wrapping. I was born wilder than she imagined. I cannot yet know to feel guilty for thriving. Having been the first to stick; for tumbling faceward into my animal exit, a brute. Neither would she know to hold me accountable, that splitting a world in two was the least of it. I would destroy her daily with my thirsty throat. They cut me free as her back arched. She would learn to void herself, spill what was left into the suckle of necessity. The meagre balance of minimum wage and her hours and her body a means. Would she have called it obeisance if the word appeared to her? If the moment had arrived for her to learn it? I suspect not, just as duty suspects a sense of volition. It is only when I am grown that they will begin to repair the mess, a hollow torn from what flesh should fill. Mesh her slackened walls. We will learn to hold her gently. A surgeon teaches us the correct measure of force: imagine an egg, then quarter it. I imagine an egg, a split, punched puzzle of grit. I want to take this story back. I cross my fingers, I leave a little gap. My fingertips against her back, I wonder which hurts most. I'm not thinking of saving my life, but of continuing to choose something biologically predetermined to leave you. Might I have loved before being born. I could not, I did not accede to a debt I will never settle. We cull a world of its resources, we gift ourselves the phrase *necessity* to palpate the twinge. Even now, fixed with this plodding consciousness I comprehend my own weight. A forest of ancient lumber falls, my chest fills up. Somebody lives. If it was her returning to this room, her face full in the cleft of my vision, I could finally ask her how to see faith ahead of fear. To be fearless enough to love with infinitude; how anybody might sift through the viscera of a violent world and look past the mess, see instead the trembling shape of something small and willing to breathe in a room that is gasping.

35

CAREN FLORANCE

Predictive text fail

I don't feel thankful|
— — — — — —

       i don't feel thankful **that**
       i don't feel thankful

The line drawing element in this visual poem tracks the letters in the phrase 'I have not been shot'. This refers to Prime Minister Scott Morrison's comments implying that participants in the March 2021 Women's March 4 Justice should be grateful not to have been met with gunfire. This poem is part of what I now call my 'case studies' practice of visual poetry, first published in *Lost in Case* (Cordite Books, 2019). I use a system based on the physical arrangement of lowercase letters in a letterpress printing case, drawing lines from letter to letter as a way of encoding difficult thoughts, feelings and above all, stories about women and the abuse directed at them. As I wrote in *Lost in Case*: 'using print to transmit these words again without re-seeding their message is a cathartic act of disruption. The results seem impenetrable, but they can, with careful attention, be restored if desired. Or not: some things are better lost.'

EUGENIA FLYNN

My skin is on the ground

Skin scraping the ground
My forehead to the ground
My hands behind my back,
hands clasped

My body sways, side to side
I push my body forward

My forehead to the ground
My hips backward to the sky
My arms behind my back

I move my body forward

The earth beneath my skin
The matter of me meets it
My brain, it tilts toward it

My grandmother's lineage
My great grandmother's mother
A thousand generations

My forehead to the ground

My mother's lineage
It meets me there
My mouth so close to earth
My breath, it goes
into the earth
the earth, into my mouth

Yellow and black
My brown skin
My skin is on the ground

My hands behind my back
My body moving forward
My skin still on the ground

ES FOONG

My Words Through Your Ears

You said in the meeting, that the female client was *hot*.
At first I don't know whether to be more offended
that you've made the first consideration
of a woman's worth — her fuckability;
or that by saying it in front of me
you think I'm clearly not.
'It's just a joke,' you say with the sideways glance
you toss in my direction.
'I'm having some fun with the boys.'
'I'm a good bloke.'
Don't mind the bitch face, boss,
I'm not going to bust your ass.
I get the joke, believe it or not,
I just don't think it's funny.
And I'm not angry, I'm just tired.

I've crafted an entire person for your consumption.
Gave myself a footy allegiance, cuss words, brass balls, the lot.
Now I can't go back in time to sign up for the MCC,
but on the whole, I think the resemblance is true,
don't you?
After all this, you have no idea how to speak to
one of your own in this other unfamiliar form.
No kids, no guns, no Range Rover,
no little lady at home to cajole
into letting me stay out the night.
To be fair, my act was never that good.
My curves too much like the lithesome strippers up there,
but with too many awkward political angles.
And I may have given myself away with one too many eye rolls
when you were just being a good bloke
and I refused to get the joke.
But honestly, I'm not angry, I'm just tired.

We were friendly so I thought we were friends.
You thought so too, because you told me the truth
When I asked the question
I didn't want the answer to:
Why do they listen to you, friend, when they don't listen to me?
Is it because I'm...?
You said, 'That might have something to do with it.'
But I've worked so hard to make my differences invisible,
I'm a man for all the important intents!
You said, 'That might have something to do with it — too.'
I should thank you for your honesty,
but I've not been able to look you in the eye.
You were a good bloke,
and stood witness to my humiliation,
and for that I can't forgive you.
You think I'm angry at you,
I'm not, I'm just tired.

When I hear my words through your ears.
When I hear the alienation but not the tears.
I can understand why you would think
the likes of me would be snatching the rice
   sorry...
      bread...
from the mouth of your babes.
And there's no use explaining that
I'm just like you, I just want to live
in the house, with the car, and the big screen tv,
and maybe do some good.
But these links are tenuous, will not bridge
the differences that run so much deeper than skin.
When you are with me,
you don't know how to be a good bloke
Believe me when I tell you,
I get the joke.
And I'm not angry, I'm just tired.

ZENOBIA FROST

'all I want is a haircut that brings me peace'

After Bec Jessen via Rhea Butcher

but you'd look pretty if we softened this
ever had a faux-hawk? let's go wild!
are you sure you want to go so short?
oh, we don't use clippers they trim too blunt
we could femme those layered lengths
you used to buzz it?! power move!
what's your man think? wish I were brave
are you... sure? are you sure you're sure?
I'm scared to snip your rebel pixie
undercut?! is this break-up hair?
so on-trend but don't you worry
you'd look a bit lez—? let's just blend that out
we could bob it? oh look new you!
cash or card today? don't you just love it!

KWEEN G
Hold the Light of Resistance

Hold the light of resistance
Resisted this resistance
We have risen
Daughters of feminism
From pioneers
We have risen
Listen
Stop
Sit in
It's a Sitting
A Fitting
Undress
Hierarchy
Anarchy of Patriarchy
Patriarchy
You don't know about me
Women Woman She
Get in your place
Get in place
Raise your horns
When she mourns
She warns
She will not do it alone
To be strong like stone
She not a stone
She the throne
The Chair
Position of Power
But not allowed, to be
To be woman
Is a Threat

The darker she gets
She's swept
Already set
To be somebody's
Subject to submit
She doesnt fit
She's not victim
She's victorious
She's wounded
The cruelty
The ruthless
Facisist
Democracy not Now
Silence and Censored
No platform to reply
To the desensitized
Renergise
With the children's cry
Will not comply
I will not
I will not
I third eye

MINDY GILL
Garden After the Fall

after The White Horse (1898) by Paul Gauguin

He is the only still point.
His colossal head bends
into the stream, chlorophyll-lit
and absolutely stoic.
A classical image –
everybody paints women and horses.
But you could miss the women:
two hunched figures smudged
into bruised foliage. Nude and nameless,
thatched into another jungled
dreamscape. Each day I come home
to find they are still trying to exit
the frame. It's my own fault:
I hung the print in the entryway hall.
I confess, I barely noticed them.
The website thumbnail so small
I saw only him – his head
like the horse of Selene's.
I unfurled the print to the reddened
strokes of pale, snake-headed petals.
The spectral branch, outstretched
like a lecherous hand. Then I saw
the second horse cut from smoked
quartz, and the third, her eye locked
on ours. What do they know?
The women cling to them forever.
It's how long the scene lasts.

ELENA GOMEZ

Venus Blood

It's a boat and we're strapped
   tight. I've got the same set
of cuffs as the rest.   You like
      to watch
how I move. As though

you could guide me. But the
ghost is my guide. She gave
us words, you know the ones,

the words of incitement, incendiary
phrases. The deep collective

Materialist immortal

Eleanor picks up the stanley knife
Eleanor pricks her finger on the stanley knife

                  We gave up on witchcraft
                  We're running down mills

Eleanor gifts a vial of Venus Blood

The ghost I told you about: she's all
Ruby billow fabric   the boat can't handle it.

We're watching the Manchester Martyrs with you

   We have a spell for the Venus Blood. It requires
Peat Pots
A flowering mint … a torn safety checklist
The severed head of a cleaning company owner or at least
   a tuft of hair

We're in the boat and our cuffs chafe. We got the fire on
standby on the banks

that ghost gift: Venus Blood

CHARMAINE PAPERTALK GREEN

Nyarlu Place Space Face

Our existence like all females originated
deep inside our grandmothers womb line
warmth of a mothers body womb holding
a seed planted deep within country
To then take a first breathe in a world where one is
Separated like on a conveyor belt into its place
The white world rejects the black and the different
And so, begins life journey of many Aboriginal women

The Nyarlu place /The Nyarlu space/The Nyarlu face

Ancestors stroke our hair at night whilst we sleep
Or when we weep and there is plenty to weep about
The babies snatched from their mothers' wombs by
DCP waiting in the birth room mothers' tears mean nothing
The children chased into police cells society racial profiling
Instilling fear whiteness aiming to break the back of a culture
The Aboriginal women dragged by an invisible bias societal force
Many fight standing strong and resist yet many do not make it

The Nyarlu place /The Nyarlu space/The Nyarlu face

Yeah, I want to talk about the women that do not make it
I want to honour their existence and reality in all of this
The ones who carry the deep wounds and scars of trauma
From their parents, their men, and a violent community of whiteness
They are told to wear it like a badge of honour because they are resilient
Because they have been brought up to live through and with trauma chaos
IF they are killed in police cells, shot on the streets or within their homes
A blinding white light saturates community's outcry of pain, loss, injustice

The Nyarlu place /The Nyarlu space/The Nyarlu face

ELOISE GRILLS

I love you so much I am ready to embrace queer death on screen

I want to die so you weep on my shirts
your sniffly nose giddy with the reminder
of our gruff bodily encounters in the crisp mountain air

I want to die from an inexplicable illness
on a bus to Miami resting my head on your shoulder
as the theme song swells one more time

I want to die being smothered by too many good things
like candelabras like rhinestones like love
and when they finally flatten my chest — it will be wonderful

I want to die being crushed
metaphorically by the weight of the prison industrial complex
also literally by a prison guard also literally by the devastating cruelty of
      TV writers

I want to die looking hot as Hilary Swank—
It's not that my life isn't worth living
It's just that your love is worth death

I wasn't doing much with my existence besides
being hot and complicated and adding colour to the main storyline
I wasn't doing much besides trying to survive

I want to die in a surprise sexual misadventure
a freak Vaseline-dyke orgy
It's not that I actually want to embrace mortality

It's just gotten so knotted up with my sexuality
It's like... calling a chocolate starfish a death star
It's like... a condom coated in cyanide

It's like...autoerotic asphyxiation
It's like a salt-soaked shirt drying stiff
in the cool mountain breeze, before it rains & rains & rains

The world floods, chandeliers are
festooned with algae; we soar to the surface like cheap violins and here I am
resting my head on your shoulder

And here I am
expiring as the first notes of our song
kick in for us

one last time

SUSAN HAWTHORNE

Bess and Surabhī

how histories are made and unmade
a tapestry of wants called needs

he said
not a single cow on the whole continent
how will we get by without milk butter cream beef?

and so they came on board with convicts
put into service while they sailed
the decks flush with dung

my name is Bess and my ancestress was on that ship
filled with Irish convicts and Irish cows
my namesake   a black Kerry   was a fine milker

when she arrived she escaped into the hills
joined with others in the unpastured scrub
ran wild and free

my friend Surabhī is a more recent arrival
shipped from Sri Lanka to join cousins
on the big stations in the north

she too escaped by avoiding the muster
which reminded her of riots and troubles at home
we met one day under a desert oak

but Surabhī's luck ran out at the next muster
they've had her under lock and key ever since

Bess in the Irish tradition is associated with the Morrigan, a shape-shifting goddess associated with death who appears as a raven and a crone, sometimes milking a cow.
    Surabhī in the Indian Hindu tradition is a bovine goddess considered the mother of all cows and the wish-fulfilling cow. She appears in many of the ancient texts including the *Mahābhārata*, the *Rāmāyana* and in Kalidasa's *Raghuvaṃśa*. Surabhī is also known as Kāmadhenu.

SARAH HOLLAND-BATT

From the Manual of Southern Cassowary Husbandry

I.

All sex ends in water.
The cassowary stalks
with her nine-iron casque
torqued high on the forehead
like a Treacy fascinator,
shakes her call across the water—
an outboard motor on choke.

As the male strays close
she stands the way women stand
when being told a lukewarm joke,
head angled in ersatz interest.

Soon she will gouge her prehistoric claws
into his shagpile coat
as he wallows in the shallows,
a cola eddy of ti-tree.

If she wanted she could rake
a single toe across his carotid artery
and leave him to bleed out
in swamp water,
tread his head down
in clay slurry.

This time, she lets him live,
shoulders his weight.

II.

Today, as she picks through greenery
for laurel, podocarp, plum,
all her thoughts are of Mondrian.

She interrupts all matrixes and perpendiculars
with wildest blue—sometimes deep
as the ocean off Mykonos
sometimes pale
as a spring azure's wing
or a reach of virgin reef.

She holds no stock in paradise.
A forest refugee, she strafes
through her new territory,
fossicks in post-cyclone towns,
jogs across the highway
to visit morning supplicants
who feed her pawpaw cubes and honeydew,
wearing their sudden interest
like a regal black gown.

III.

Certain rituals should not be heeded.
Thankless childrearing, for example.
She takes lovers when she pleases,
dispatches them when they have finished pleasing.

Fruit she swallows whole
for the swagger of engulfing whole planets.

Her young she scatters as sage green eggs in the scrub.
This is not unusual in the animal kingdom.
When they meet again she may murder them
the way you might drive a carful of children
into a lake
the way you might hold a blanket
over each face,
righteous and full of rage,
to make some point about mothering.

LK HOLT
Category Error

The monks of Mount Athos chant
                we've died
                and fallen in love
                with everything.
A sublime deformation of preference
is possible, when the whole virgin half-isle
is theirs and claustral, free
of domestic females for millennia,
weekly eggs and milk trucked in
far from a body's temperature.
(It doesn't take a lot of sustenance
to love what is promised.)

The female mouser, while in winter
hard to keep wild, isn't yet
the category error, despite how long
she loves the door upright,
despite the thorn of *How is a body*
a caress?, despite the thorn of pleasure.

ZEINA ISSA

The Midwife

I remember your hands, dandelion clock
soft, like the gentle descent of snowflakes
on Mount Sannine. Plump as fresh-baked

khubz, I would tuck myself into
your flank—my snuggling potion.
Now, I long for the *when* of how things were,

for the Beqaa Valley tessellating from the veranda
and the trailing, summer grapevine arbor
guarding your grandchildren's giggles.

I ache for winter's cherries in sickly sweet syrup
and your home-made labne balls dipped in *zaatar*
hidden far from our ravenous reach.

Your midwifery tales did not wane with your moonlight hair.
Motherless young, widowed young, you carved pillars
out of your ribs of sorrow and kindled

life from life, swallowing a woman's bellow
whole when *push* became a deafening echo.
Out of womb cocoons, babies were pulled

bathed and anointed with olive oil. Swaddled
in cotton white, you held them like mother-earth
holds onto her roots.

In a sunken valley of razed memories
in the fertile land of Zahle and Baalbek—
your Astarte light pellucid.

ELEANOR JACKSON
Nominated intimacy

in this way I resolve myself
to the deep loneliness of marriage
between a man and a woman
at too close proximity
bodies stalemating one another
yet strangely alert to motion
always traces of the other
a hat, some shoes, a glass grubby with prints
grateful for the toddler
her observable existence
baby in utero for capacious company
beginner's knees against ribs
to remind you
alone is both relative and
deeply desired
we do not talk for talking is not his thing
only mine and mind alone
what does it matter?
the other will always do as they have
intended to do
love to their ignorant limits
pre-agreed or otherwise
the contract even
in its part performance
can be enforceable
bitterness surges with the weather foul
trapped indoors cleaning
or preparing to clean
open to the sunshine escaping
the inevitable repetitions and
practices of steadfast commitment
no longer afraid of humiliation
now that I am a certified houswyf

LIZZIE JARRETT

#unapologeticallywoman

Dedicated to the patriarchy that try to keep us oppressed...
Remember you are birthed from a woman's vagina and nurtured
        from a breast...
Why are women still needing to prove our worth...
When we create life through child birth.
Carrying the next generations to walk this earth.
Yet one day of recognition is all we deserve??
Though even if we do not become mothers,
The strength of women stands above all others!
For we are the ones that unconditionally love and care,
The weight of the world our shoulders do bear...
Without us the truth is men could not succeed,
For their life is created when we bleed...
Embrace the matriarchy and all its worth
The essential blessings of mother earth.

JILL JONES

These Deeds of a Woman

If I'm exhausted, I'm still beautiful
like a dying tree, a pretty weed
a purple flower fluttering like plastic in a gutter.
I bend with earth not prophecy
though sometimes prophecy sleeps with me.
The toughness of an old hand
is what paradise might feel like.

Walking is a deed that unfolds me
a line of a poem, a bee buzzing with
nectar calculus, a handful of wire or rope.

I'm swept up in each minute of work and pitch.
I drive a truck, lead a horse.
I tidy hair or a set of tools on a bench
sing an ovation to the food of every sex.

Age is a cloud sometimes, it hides
the disputatious light, or helps me sleep
as if bluer than the past, secure as a gate
shaky as the back fence.
I've had a long conversation with night
its protections, its blows, its recumbent noise.

I welcome the bright famous moonlight
the shades of evening's voluptuous demeanour
the morning that's ecstatic with
every leaf of air.

I walk alongside you, and my shoulder
and my senses.
Half the sky follows me
half of it is ahead.

GABRIELLE JOURNEY JONES
Portable Lives

Some houses have an entire junk room
We only have room for junk boxes
Treasured chests and old suitcases
Salvaged from the shipwreck of separation
Containers of collected experiences.

Like the eventual death of our family
Station wagon, all of her familiar contents
Swept into a coffin of a cardboard box
Memorialised now beside my bed
Hidden with six others underneath
An ink-stained rainbow tablecloth
Storage imitating furniture perfectly
Balancing a lamp, scrap paper and a leaky pen.

There is a plastic box crammed with school reports
Notebooks, kindergarten drawings and newsletters
Memories held for my children to enjoy
When we have a permanent place to unpack.
Another tattered box rattles with rainy day activities
Miscellaneous things like old jewelry and crystals
Messy art supplies, birthday cards and missing keys
Overcrowded with creativity and melancholy.

Three other cartons remain sealed
Four decades folded up carefully
Our portable lives held closely
Inside these precious junk boxes
Waiting for us to find home and safety.

'Portable Lives' is a glimpse into what we hold, waiting to unpack and settle after separation and domestic violence. Many women take years to finally find home and rebuild their lives.

JEANINE LEANE

On International Women's Day

This year like every other the white women will
come out to celebrate Women's Day.
There'll be purple ribbons, T-shirts, banners, flags
slogans saying Women of the World Unite—
there'll be corporate breakfasts, achievement awards,
champagne and motivational speakers.

You're just like us
the white women at my work tell me when I
decline their invitation to celebrate. *Just like us...
only... well... we're all the same under the skin.*
They tell me not ask me.
Between my skin and my womanhood
and my womanhood and my skin are blood and bone.
My skin is blak. Inside is my womanhood.
Do I peel my skin from my body or wrench my body from my skin?
Either way feminism will make me bleed.

I was destined Blak and conceived woman.
I am neither Blak only nor woman alone.
I have too many Sistas without happy endings
too many Aunties who've hit the wall
seen too many Mothers weep for lost children
know too many women who will only wear purple
in bruises on their faces and bodies
to celebrate this day.

CARISSA LEE

tall poppy town

As buildings turn to grassy fields,
freeway turns to single road,
the knot in my stomach turns to acidic heaviness
and I wonder what the fuck I'm doing here.

Driving down the highway we walked,
we were fifteen and the sun was coming up.
Young ones on adventures in hazy houses and cold parks.
It was safer then.
This town now littered
with old people, junkies, and women in activewear.
Streets lined with empty shop fronts,
hopeful hipster cafes for the youth left behind.

No trace of brave, happy academic,
respected, loved and fought for.
All that I've trudged through and achieved
shrivels and sheds off me like sunburn
every time you bring me here.

This place is cold ground, harsh air and outdated humour,
and you make me come back to it.
your brother let her be buried here,
and now we're tethered here like a haunting.
He hit you in a flat on Bertha Street
and your babies came to your rescue
we drive past that street to get to your house.
why do you make me come back here?

You trauma-bonded with a place
that beat you up,
called your kids "coon"
assaulted your daughter
and kicked your son to keep him down.

Merry Christmas

KATE LILLEY

Wrongs of Woman (after Mary Wollstonecraft)

Sentiments blotted out

> *A blank space about ten characters in length*

wormed [the whole of]

> *note the omission of any*
> *allusion to that circumstance*

embedded account: adversity, propensity
skirts the metropolis

One of the -- passing heard my tale
sequel of a dismal story
> *back to my hole*

Accidental converse
brutes I met
> *do not start – dismission --*

She sent him the memoirs written for –
remarks necessary to elucidate
my project of usefulness

Dead heart of a libertine
squalid object

> *an episode seems to have been intended*
> *never committed to paper*

Bastilled – if women have a country –
no debts of mine [fair Roxana]

I forgot to mention --
****
****
****
> *unruffled lake*

BRONWYN LOVELL
Killer

Ever since I encountered the bikie
who complimented my eyes and
tried to fondle me at a rest stop
on the Western Highway, I have
wanted a Doberman called Killer.

When I called for my dog that day,
voice shaking as I quickstepped
back to the car, her name did not
seem threatening enough; it was
Labrador lovely, Whippet weak.

Carmela was too sweet in her pink
diamante collar devoid of studs.
Forty kilometres down the road,
sure I was not being followed,
I pulled over and rang my dad.

He said I should expect to be hit
on by men because I was young
and pretty. I've aged now and
put on some weight, so maybe
I'm safe. I still want a Doberman.

I would spell her name K-H-I-L-A,
which means 'blooming' in Hindi.
I've always thought having a dog
would protect me, but it didn't
shield Toyah Cordingley. Her dad

found her gentle Shepherd Indie
tied to a tree not far from her naked
body. Toyah was too pretty to walk
carefree along a quiet beach with
a dog that was not a killer — her

youth blooming, legs moving, heart
beating fast as her bare feet quick-
stepped across the sand, smiling
in that I-am-no-threat way, before
being hit on under the beaming sun.

MELISSA LUCASHENKO

Screaming Blue Murder

They found a woman in a ditch the other day
A dead woman in a ditch the other day
A dead Asian woman in a ditch the other day
A dead Asian bride in a Logan ditch the other day

And when they found – (they: two vomiting schoolchildren) – a dead Asian
Filipino bride in a ditch the other day they found:

The dead Filipino bride of a Queensland policeman
The murdered Filipino bride of a Queensland policeman
The pregnant Filipino bride of a senior Queensland policeman.

And when they found (they: the public) the pregnant Filipino bride of a senior
Queensland policeman, they found:

That white Australian hears Filipino women only from the degradation
    of ditches
That the thin blue line is a black and blue rope around the necks of murdered
    minority women
That just comes for us not in uniform, but in costume.

And when they found (they: you) the pregnant murdered Filipino bride of a
senior Queensland policeman, they found:
what the poor, and women, and people of colour have always known
and will continue to tell
until you listen
to our living voices,
not our bodies
lying in ditches,
murdered
by the side of the road.

JENNIFER MAIDEN
Diary Poem: Uses Of Iron Ladies

Violence. Ambition. Bitterness. Lust, not so much. In the recent faction
series *The Crown* (what on earth are they going to say about Sir Richard
Dearlove, Princess Diana and the Alma Tunnel Cameras?) Denis Thatcher
observes of his wife Margaret and the Queen that England is being run by two
menopausal women, asks what could go wrong. Well, for a start, with Thatcher:
the Poll Tax, the destruction of unions, and the Falklands Battle. But a proper
question here, from a feminist point of view is whether the conservative use
of women with warlike tastes is against the nature of women or whether it just
acknowledges natural deadliness in the female of the species. Hillary Clinton
crowing about sodomised Gaddafi is what in my poetry finally reduces
Eleanor Roosevelt now to limbolike Bardo traumatised. It's hard to make this
lyrical, although I suppose there is always something lyrical about knives:
the manner in which they scatter light back but still seem to have their own
bright vector. Biden's cabinet of women are all warlike, tended to support
the Iraq invasion, be heavily involved with complexes Military and Industrial.
It wears thin using Identity Politics for them, as for Gillard, when she wanted
to remove Assange's passport, reduced the poignant pensions of Single
Mothers, came up with the Malaysian Solution. Is there anyone amongst them
who would not sink the retreating Belgrano, it out of territorial bounds, it
youngly full of bewildered South Americans? I've often written on differences
between Pankhursts: Emmeline and Christabel recruiting for WW1 and Sylvia
against it. Are you Emmeline or Sylvia? The ALP is full of ostensibly left-wing
women on the make with the U.S. Democrats, who hate Assange for knowing
about Seth Rich. Gillard comforts comfortably on the Brookings team, no
doubt 'ubique' – their motto – at Foreign Relations Council. On her inconstant
lap top, Ghislaine Maxwell has much more daily time on a constant laptop
than Assange and is not exposed to Covid. The Irish have a marriage proposal:
'Do you want to be buried with my people?' Freud said his last unanswered
question was 'What do women want?' but let's ask what men want: to trust
the mother? To trust the mother to do what? Protect the species, annihilate
other children in the playground? And is that what the mother wants, or does
she want all children, and their mothers to confide in? Boudica in her knived

chariot, bright on biteable coins, has voted for Brexit, but so would Thatcher.
And the European Union marbled up Greece. There is that for self-isolation,
the lightning-rod on its solitary steeple. But the lightning Glenda Jackson in
British Parliament made a speech about the death of Thatcher, saying that,
yes, Thatcher was a woman, but 'That isn't my idea of a woman.' Men in
power have learned to lie, to run, too much or not enough, depending
on a reflection. And finishing here would you choose which evil:
to lie alone, to lie, or to be buried with my people?

SELINA TUSITALA MARSH

Mother's Machete

was found
growing in weeds

at the foot of a
palm tree

busting out of a
too-small washing

machine barrel
she'd stabbed

it neck-deep
in the soil

like she always
used to do

its bloody pouliuli blade
burnt with rusting earth

its shark teeth ripped
back and forth

her nifo'oti

she skimmed the top
off soured

milk and honey
migrant dreams

then wiped its tip
on her housedress

before donning
heels and stepping out

to siva afi
on white suburban dance floors

we'd find machetes
all over our house

thrust through deck planks
impaling garage walls

biting the stone driveway
perhaps for our safety

she kept it out
of arm's reach

more likely
it was a warning

reminding us
no matter

how fast
the runner

winter or summer
gutless

or full of honour
knowing or full of wonder

hunted or the hunter
stunned or the stunner

a machete mother
is always faster.

Samoan words
Pouliuli: An existential darkness
Nifo'oti: Ceremonial war club
Siva Afi: Fire dance

JENNIFER KEMARRE MARTINIELLO

Being My Grandmothers (After Uluru)

I recovered a reverberation of sounds from the rocks/the red earth/from the paleo river scars/from beaches like *Kamay* ... half-buried in the quicksand

of forgetfulness ... half-disinterred to be rematriated like Ancestral remains ancient in-my-blood sounds/lost/taken under the blanket suffocations of colonial

history for unheard/unheeded   yet enduring   un-muffled   echoing ... in my children's throats/in my grandchildren's throats/whispering/singing

resurrecting an archaeology of lost sounds/the first ceremonies/ the first lullabies/hunting songs and whale songs/laughter and healing songs

Creation stories and True Stories/a heritage of grandmothers' voices millennia long speaking with Uluru's ... a genealogy of words/once spoken/forever

echoing in my throat/in my children's throats/in my grandchildren's throats... I retrieved a broken word today, picked it up off the ground where it had been

thrown away/carelessly like an empty plastic bottle/a bit crushed like an utterance might crack with emotion between a vowel and a consonant of a word once

meant to be whole/a container of meaning and substance/integrity to sustain futures like water might quench drought and thirst/nourish and give life but can't because

someone who didn't know/didn't understand/didn't respect this place / this Law
thought it wasn't relevant/that it didn't have a use/ a meaning/a place   thought

it didn't belong same way they didn't belong to this place/where words are sacred/are
covenants/not defiled/dismembered/re-purposed for political convenience

I heard a bloodless sound after Uluru/a string of words like stones bereft
of spirit/heart/life/without skin or pulse to render its speakers worthy of belonging/

worthy to be keepers of the Rule of Law…
denial is a chasm two and a half centuries deep/the wound-salted erosion

of the land/of our bodies/of our soul/the induced deprivation of an ecology where
'absence' and 'truth' occur in the same sentence without parole or redemption

After Uluru: *The Uluru Statement: Voice, Treaty, Truth*
Kamay: *Eora* name for Botany Bay

SO MAYER
Tally

/ and to say that we / are generation ships we
are not / increase not metaphor but memory
bellied forth we / do not carry gametes only
do not inherit just / for all its sparkle / chemistry
we do it / more like moon amoeba on a go-slow
no boobs or boobs / agogo proliferating / through
mouths bowed like cellos such / sweet stoma
whose openings we / piercing / slip through
need or needle stitching spacetime / fabric
up close & porous / how we turn telescopic
inhale centennial pollution & / release / speak
grammar of sky uncynicised every second
is a chance a chance / a chance to start over
every second is a / once upon a new origin
story curtain / on a second act hear that / ovation
o o we are so close o o come on now o open
up

TEENA MCCARTHY

where have the Bush Marys gone?

I will no longer hide
The truth of the Bush Marys
She is the Non virgin
Used by the carnal

She her body
She is her blood
She has no voice
She comes out of the bush
She comes out of dark
She comes out of the light
She returns to the dark

She is the mother of the bush
She is the Holy ghost

JAZZ MONEY

I don't sleep anymore

I don't sleep anymore
instead I feast with my arms
deep to the elbows
in the primordial stickiness of hope
from it I pull many fevered sicknesses
and a constant series of doors
but it's not like the metaphor where a window opens
it's more like a dimensionless maze
and some hydra beast

I don't sleep anymore
instead I plant seeds throughout the moon garden
and wait for my children to rise up
from the twin wombs in our bed
the place where I whisper and chant
for peace

I don't sleep anymore
instead I dream of places where I can step upon the ground
and not hear the cries of my kin rising from the blood soaked earth
shrinking beneath a mean sky

no I don't sleep anymore
I just weep and weep
until I turn back
to a river

no I don't sleep anymore
now I wander through the smoke plume
inhaling the dust of that
long distant explosion

I don't sleep anymore
instead I dance with my eyelids
deep to the moon
in the sun of primordial stickiness
from it I pull many fevered children
and a constant many coloured glass
~~but it's n~~ot like the metaphor where a path forks
but more like an ailing animal
forgetting pain

I don't sleep anymore
instead I shake dust throughout the dream garden
and cry for my children against time
from the seeds in our hearts
the place where I spin and spin
and weep

I don't sleep anymore
instead I visit places where I can step with the ancestors
and find peace in my kin rising from the earth
hoping beneath an endless breeze

no I don't sleep anymore
I just laugh and laugh
until I turn back
to a bird

no I don't sleep anymore
now I wait for you upon the shore
inhaling the oyster shells of that
long distant ocean

LORNA MUNRO

Snake skins

We are beautiful only for a short time.
Everyone worried about that shit fading
while I'm here patiently waiting for the
fourth time and hoping I am more than
my appearance in that birth line.
I am more than how a man views me
from the outside in.
I am more than what you see truly.
I am carrying weight in bones and
my blood is unruly just like my hair.
And I just don't give a fuck that you stare
I will stare straight back down cos I wasn't
born to appease you. I wasn't born to please you
or your foreign ideas of beauty.

I wasn't born to stay silent, beguiled
or tamed cos you think I'm wild.
Black woman walks this earth to fulfill the
grandmothers' curse of not giving in,
continually raising children to see that
colours mean much more than what you see
there is meaning to everything created in
this world so why do we refuse to lean in
and accept the ageing, the knowing and the
growing of our own beauty?
Coveted beside these aliens for all they are
worth they are pretty.

I am magnificent, ancient.
They are consumed while I drive the stake in
these very words leaving all artificial add-ons
for the taking.
Cos I am fine with my old age
and snakeskins.

DIANTY NINGRUM

If I die *to my rainforest sisters*

I could be, for example, your favorite tree. I could be your country
—her most gentle tyrant. Coins of merchants in your silent,
foreign bazaar. A jar of no-name black tea with a hint of sweetness from itself. It sounds manic to list the shapes we no longer embody:
worker, daughter, believer. The shell with cotton veil. The wall
that paints itself. The color grey. Ambivalent as a tongue, unbitten.
If I should move I won't move like water. No more dismembering. The
offbeat nods of a parrot despite the crowd—almost a life worthy like a holy
zeal. I could be today's momentary aubade. I'd glide a hue darker, numbing
like everyday's casual cruelties. Like wind that contours edges. No more
thorny kindness. I could be just you—Reformation's beloved casualties.
No more citadel reserved for every entitled man. So long, the ebbing years
that keep entertaining the anthropocene—each passing like rotten elegance.
This body's a lake to mourn your shredded beauty. Like you, grief surrenders
in certain ways. Grief sings its own song. No grave deep enough for every
grief. Say, to love your people is to survive—my people, dare I say I survive
a violent love despite decades of decaying? My people, have you tried dying
in silence? Die some more & die again a thousand times, each death annulled
by its remembrance. If someone dies, sisters, may roses bleed. May we be
given whatever suffices. A body that withstands. The lone song that carries
weight. Hushed chirp in the distance. This land, wet as it is.

This poem is a lamentation in solidarity with women of the palm oil plantation in the rainforest of Sumatra and Kalimantan who were raped, abused, and severely underpaid for years. A recent investigation uncovered the gross violence behind the industry that at the same time has produced beauty products for women elsewhere.

MAUREEN JIPYILIYA NAMPIJINPA O'KEEFE
What Is A Feminist?

I am not sure how to tell my story as a feminist.
You tell me what is a feminist.
I am a woman. I am my mother's daughter.
My mother's youngest daughter.
I was born with this name...
Maureen Jipyiliya Nampijinpa O'Keefe
I am Kateye Walpiri woman from my mother's side.
I write as I talk.
I talk as I think.
I think a lot about the woman who gave me my name.
Molly Nungarrayi O'Keefe.
The story of Maureen starts with my mother, Molly.
Molly was a bush therapist.
Not a bush doctor but a bush therapist.
Mum had special ways about her.
The bush was her home.
Her stories were my home too.

Through my mother's name everybody tells me
O'Keefe is Irish.
I like that. I like that a lot.
Ever since I was a little girl, I would go to the library
at the Ali-Curung School and read about Ireland.

A four-leaf clover land covered in green.
Funny little men with orange beards.
Different from the red central deserts
of my homelands.

Molly was a dressmaker with hessian bags
empty of flour and wheat she could make anything.
Mum would make dresses and pants for

our people who were coming into to town
from bush so that they had something to wear
in public.
Does this make her a dressmaker?
I think so.

*Yawulyu** – body painting design for woman's dance group.
Mum was a bush composer, singer, and dancer.
Molly moved her body in harmony with the
trees and their songs.

A long time ago, my Mum would ride on
horseback to collect the royal mail and parcels
 from Barrow Creek
and take it back to Wauchope Hotel
in days gone by they would refer to this line
of work as the Pony Express.
In a man's world my Mum moved the mail.
But that is enough about me.
Please tell me, what is a feminist?

*Yawulyu** – sacred woman's dance

SUNEETA PERES DA COSTA
Roses

If we could go back – which we can't –
I would be waiting on the doorstep,
face warming in the winter sun as
she cut and wrapped overblown roses.
Unlike other mothers, who'd make
decorative aluminium foil bouquets,
her gift to the teacher was issued in
reused butcher's paper. Embarrassed,
I took them from her careful hands;
kissing her quickly, worried about
missing the bus, about being late, being
noticed – but also longing to be seen.
I carried them loosely, lest the thorns
came through, new teeth – little sabres –
ready to bite the hand that fed etcetera.
When they pricked my fingers, I lay
them on my lap. Mistake, mistake! For,
studious as a naturalist, I could see
numerous small bugs had died or become
stranded in the filaments and the reused
paper was stained with lamb's blood...
Lamb of God, who takes away the sins of
the world? I wondered, sustaining injuries
to fingertips. The bus lurched and I tried
to hang on, although the sandwiches –
mortification of cucumber, cheese and
chutney! – were now done for. If there was
a lesson or allegory I learnt it much later.
For example, I should never, ever let the
blood show or stain my uniform; that,
regardless of prayer, or virtue, harm could
come to me and I could do it too. Love was

this perpetual leap of faith, wrapped in layers
tainted with doubt, gift without expectation
or regret. This body, sacred if not quite holy,
could bruise easily. Thorns were prickles,
epidermal parts of the rose finding traction.
And within me too, though I was still quite
unware of it, were hips, bud, petals, anthers,
ovaries – stigmata of her blighted gift to me.

RENEÉ PETTITT-SCHIPP

Southern Right Whale with Calf

(after Aldo Leopold)

(I)

Morning   between the point
and the mountains
the whale lifts her fins to the sun
dual dark sails   the raised reef
of her body

calf masked as shadow – warp
and trace – until surface breaks as tail
tastes new air

morning   and the whale is thinking
with the sea   like a mountain.
She lifts her fins to the sun
twin dark peaks   the raised reef
of her body.

(II)

In my sleep I hear the whale moan
the sound of her rising over sedge and dune
under star and shifting shape of cloud
a tuba of sorrow   low brass of bliss
piped sigh heavy with history

it pulls me from half-felt dreams
to share a swell of polar darkness
to rock like mothers do in dead of night
to sing like mothers do in dead of night
deep belief in the promise
of morning.

ANUPAMA PILBROW

Still Life of Flesh Wound Under Big Tree Poem

One morning I am feeling quite angry
and I am going for an angry walk and
I am picking up all the broken bits of
glass and corroding batteries bent nails
and big rocks as many as I can get my
angry little hands on and I am shoving
them into a very finely wrought silver
mesh sack creating simply a formidable
weapon which I am carrying like a small
and pretty clutch. I am walking into the
centre of the city until I find the Big Tree
and I am standing below it smiling
and looking very pretty with my fine
silver purse bulging suggestively with
dangerous secret items in fashionable
sharp angles. In the shade of the Big
Tree I am handing out all secret delights
from my secret purse I take one one
rock one glass sliver and press them
each into the grubby hands of passersby
until our palms are raw and open
and touching. Their filth is in my blood
and my blood is in theirs and I give
away my own little anger in exchange
for absorbing the contaminated exudate
of each open palm no longer am I feeling
so angry simply weak and poisoned
from blood loss.

FELICITY PLUNKETT

Springturn

Split the day's skin,
singing. Jimmy
the window open – light
drifts in. Night folds
back. Dissolves. Buds

fuzz, unfold. Leaves
lean into your sill, bladed
with light. Dark has no
hold. Butterflies
begin again. The gate clicks –

loosens its tongue. Blossom
tingles along bone
branches. Colours itch. Spring hitches
her skirt, steps over the sleeping
dog in your hall, all

her gifts aflame. Spills
across your kitchen: story
of seed, story of petal, story
of frith and axil. Heat rushes
in – pulse, hush.

Uncurl your limbs. Night
has gone, winter
falls away. Let go
your habits of cold, habits
of sorrow, flicker of affliction.

Draw the blind. Look out:
she laughs seedlings
into being. Pour
your soul, pour again
all that thaws now spring is

with you: blood, songs
you thought you'd
forgotten. Only the calm dark
now, the shade you rest with,
console. Surprise wakes

in you: tingles
your skin. She's come
to share with you songs
she's stored, let loose
blossoms along trees'

bones. Lift the curtain, lift
winter's hem, lift
with the night. Spring scents
days that follow
the fallow, blinking in light.

ANNE POELINA WAGABA

First Law: Matrix or Patrix

Deconstructing the Patrix is not about confusing the Matrix
What has COVID19 taught us as human beings?
Where has the greed of the predatory elite taken us
Can we pause and take a deeper breath?
Can we Dream…new Dreams, in this modern Dreamtime?

Rebellion Extinction people believe if the humans are so stupid…befall their own demise
Mother Earth will right size herself.
I pause only for one short moment, before I replied.
Yes, Mother Earth can heal and transform herself…but…
She will be lonely with the vibrations of Human and non-Human Beings.

2021 Chinese New Year of the Metal Ox
COVID19 what has our world taught us.
The place we work, we live, we love…we die on
We each one of us have a relational earth bond
Maybe because each and every one of us are Indigenous to Mother Earth.

We cannot continue to devour Mother Earth
To disrespect living energy systems
We cannot continue the fossil fuels graveyards across her girth
Destroying the amazing Amazon at an alarming rate
Our atmospheres are collapsing
We have gone down into the oceans burying carbon, destroying deep seabed life.
My wise women want to know for …'whose greater good?'
Are we muted from crying out, Sing …Sing.. the songlines that have carried our bloodlines…..more than 7 generations to come.

'THESE EARTH SYSTEMS NEEDS TO BE VALUED, LOVED…RELATIONAL AND RECOGNISED!'

Love, an ethics of care, sharing in a circular economy, these are the values for reframing reclaiming and celebrating life
One of fusion of human, social, cultural, environmental capital
Yes...some form of currency, for trade for sharing our reciprocal economy

Feminism is not about othering Masculinism.
It's a fusion which requires, ethics of care of love of bravery.
Being Brave is what is required to be a good and decent Human Being
The Power is within you, you are Human Being.

Dream your own actuality, be who you want to be but most importantly
Be the sacred gift of life for ALL Life.
Multispecies justice...there is no 'othering'
Birds, fish, insects, flowers, bush bees, snakes and lizards with others amongst the grass.
Sameness in value of life between human and non-human beings
Not Matrix deconstructing Patrix
First Law, Law of the Land
A Declaration of Interdependence
Multispecies Justice of Land, Living Waters for Mother Earth's Peoples and kin
Wholeness and Wellbeing, communityism, regionalism, pluralism, sameness not difference.

First Law... It's time to redefine who we are?

Nyikina Warrwa Yimardoowarra Marnin

MEL REE

'3rd world mumma'

my mother's eyes are a cloudy grey
her mother wailed the colour away

when she died in her arms
she was twelve years old

she buried the pain in her pupils
she buried a mother
a son
buried a daughter
buried parts of herself

when she held their heavy, lifeless bodies for the last time
her arms a temporary coffin
my mother's skin stained with grief
her hands hunger to hold my baby brother's once more
to stroke my sister's hair
her hands hang heavy with sorrow

burdened boulders have shaped canyons on my back
crashing into bones

grief would sink from skin to vein
vein to heart
producing toxic waste
thump thump thump
anger spills through fist
through face
my mother's heart produced toxicity
anger coursing through with primal intensity
which came from grief
she never dealt with
horrors black women from third worlds
have to deal with
they are modern day warriors
that's some real shit

my mother's hair
full
used too many times
like a leash
to throw her across the room

each tightly woven titanium curl
holds secrets to sin
unfathomable
subjected to fear filled hate
from her own kin
survived living conditions
incomprehensible

finally awoken a woman

instead of seeing poor village girl
pikinini from Papua New Guinea
I SEE my mother
mama blo me
I see an ancient spirit
demonic
divine

descendant of warriors
sorcerers
primitive bloodline
instead of seeing mistakes
I flip the script

see what it took
what it takes
when you've got nothing
and still
remove foot off the brake
with sheer will

make
it to the next day break
with every horizon
give thanks

the only proof you're alive
sun beams striking your skin
honey brown sparkling melanin

NEGAR REZVANI

Silent Suffering   Translated by Saba Vasefi

Like a wounded tree
that burned
in the fire of the Island's feverish forests
and the only cure for its blisters
are dark clouds,
I have fallen in love with the rain
which has reduced the probability
of burning my 25-year-old
leaves below zero
and swallowing prison moulds.

For the wind,
for human rights,
for politics,
there is no trust —
Wherever the tongueless fire explodes
and silent suffering sits in its ashes
they arrive to give aid:
not to save lives,
but to facilitate deaths.

Just like the wind
that blows the fire
fiercer and faster
they are twisting around
the throat of my displacement
to announce the destruction
of this bruised and lifeless soul.

Life is a strange incident;
but the life of an outcast is an even
more horrible hospital

prescribing Cyanide
to its injured patients,
and its nurses are rugged men
who ruthlessly steal the pillow
of peace from under our heads.

Where everything is wild
even light is a prisoner,
and justice commits suicide every day.

But here
you can only fall in love with the rain
which keeps life crisp and delicate.
So long live the rain
that gives life to my leaves
so that my poems may take root again.

رنج خاموش
نگار رضوانی

مثل درختی زخمی
که در آتش جنگل های تب دار جزیره
سوخته
و تنها مرهم تاول هاش ابرهای تیره اند
دل به باران سپرده ام
که احتمال
احتراق برگ های بیست و پنج سال ساله ام را
به زیر صفر رسانده
و کپک های زندان را می بلعد.

به باد
به حقوق بشر
به سیاست
هیچ اعتمادی نیست

هرکجا که آتش بی زبانی زبانه می کشد
و رنجی بی صدا به خاکستر می نشیند
برای امداد می رسند
امداد نه برای نجات
نه برای زندگی
برای تسهیل مرگ

درست مثل باد که می پیچد میان آتش
تا زودتر
و کاری تر بسوزاند
دور گلوی آوارگی هایم انقدر چنبره می زنند
تا ویرانی جان کبود و بی نفس ام را اعلام کنند.

زندگی اتفاق عجیبی است
اما
ویلانی بیمارستانی است هولناک تر
که به بیماران مجروحش
سیانور تجویز کرده

و پرستارانش مردانی تنومند
که بی رحمانه بالش آرامش را
از زیر سر ما می دزدند.

جایی که همه چیز وحشی است
سپیدی زندانیست
و عدالت هر روز خودکشی می کند
این جا
فقط می شود عاشق باران شد
که ترد و ظریف زندگی را زنده نگه می دارد

پس زنده باد باران
که به برگ هایم جان می دهد
تا شاید شعرهایم دوباره ریشه زنند

LYNETTE RILEY

*I Am – birthed, born, directed, learnt, learned,
strong & strengthened*

I am birthed in this Country entwined in Kinship and spiritual connections to the Land and its environment.
I am birthed by hundreds of thousands of years and generations of history, knowledges, learnings and philosophical beliefs which make me one with this Country our Mother.
I am birthed in the indoctrination of colonisation which denied and sought to destroy our magnificent Cultures, as they use our Countries resources and tear it apart.
I am birthed in a long line of strong women and men, who fought to maintain their identity, cultures and languages with great joy and deep sorrow.
I am birthed in a struggle for maintaining our souls and Connections to Country.

I was born into a Kinship network so strong that colonisation cannot break it.
I was born into a network of grandmothers, grandfathers, mothers and fathers who held me aloft, so that I might grow strong in culture.
I was born into my Nations to shine a light on who we are.
I was born to be a spokesperson and challenge colonisation.
I am born to ensure we continue in our own right.

I have been directed by my old people to learn western education.
I have been directed by my old people to challenge and change this education.
I have been directed by my old people to maintain my own cultural traditions.
I have been directed by my old people to help teach cultural traditions.
I am directed by my old people.

I was born a girl to learn from my mothers.
I was born a girl to learn from my fathers.
I was born a girl to learn anything is possible.
I was born a girl to prove everything is possible.
I was born a girl to demonstrate strength.

I have learnt Kinship and family is everything.
I have learnt western education is just one tool.
I have learnt Connections to Country are my foundations.

I have learnt suffering makes me stronger.
I have learnt my strength for my children and grandchildren.

I have learned to teach.
I have learned to love.
I have learned to hate.
I have learned to survive.
I have learned.

I am strong in my identity.
I am strong in my family.
I am strong in my Connection to Country.
I am strong in my culture.
I am strong.

I am strengthened by Country, sheathed in its continuity.
I am strengthened by my Family, those who have come before and those who come after me.
I am strengthened by my Kinship connections, whose responses to racism, hate and colonialism have taught me.
I am strengthened by my cultural practices, which maintain my integrity and identity.
I am strengthened.

SAMAH SABAWI

Case # 70

That's not how I imagined it would be
Legs parted on the blood-soaked dirt
Strangers rolling up my skirt
Hands pulling down my undies
Guns and phones pointing at me
UN observers counting indignities
They write me down
They write me down
They write me down a number
I am case # 70
69 women gave birth at checkpoints
69 women before me
Not one... Not two... Not three
I am case # 70
I inhale strength and sumud and exhale their cruelty
I'm not a stray animal to be left on the dirt
The ambulance is here for me
I booked a hospital room
I decorated a nursery
I push... I push... I push
Can I have some privacy?
I am case # 70
I inhale the wisdom of a thousand matriarchs
And the patience of a million refugees
And I exhale fear and tyranny
I am case #70

I inhale the scent of lemon
The fragrance of jasmines
The warmth of your skin
The tenderness of your flesh
Slipping out of me
And into a spectacle of inhumanity
This is not how I imagined it would be
I breathe you in
And breathe them out
I breathe out the tanks and guns
The human rights conventions
The UN resolutions
The bullshit conferences
All of it fades into nothingness
Until you and I are all there is
Until all there is ... is you and me
We are case # 70

SARA M. SALEH

The (Not So) Secret Life of 3arab Girls: Our Raqs is Sharqi

An intermittent Ghazal   *(After Patricia Smith)*

They can't stop us 3arab girls, spring coil curls, sentimental lines of kohl, hums, hollers, and trills, *Allah, Allah*, dropping our raqs sharqi.

Stepping out in scarves and tassels, strong backs we strut and swing, on streets, at weddings, in living rooms, chest to chest, pot belly to pot belly.

The record skips, belt up them wide hips, henna night is vibin'. *Aweeeeha, glory be to our pure bride*, her teta ululates, *li li li*.

Drums thump, sweaty, stretchmarked thighs rub, shame at our feet, tonight I am not difficult to love, watch these sides shake and shimmy.

Gears whirring, grinding, blazing, *ya banat, glide up that galabeya*, dip like Tahia, Samia, and Hind, swerve those curves on that God-given body.

They can't stop us 3arab girls, dancing til fajr interrupts, swatting white 'belly dancers' in genie pants gyrating unceremoniously.

Mothers and daughters and sisters and beloveds, slide on over, and slide it good. Give thanks to the Divine as we revive the sacred raqs, raqs sharqi.

KIRLI SAUNDERS
Sacred Women Ways

I remember the day we met
   I eyed you shyly
      unsure of how your magic might arrive

         I watched it fly right by me
            pulling me in to a safe place of growth
              and you showed me how to go
                the old way
                   slowly and kind

                          since, I've been trying to do the same
                      for our young ones
                            to channel those sacred women's ways
                      as you do
                          you know the way

you always knew the way

               to stay just as bold and grounded
          to follow guidance
         to hone defiance
       for anything less than what's best
     for our people

in the process of my becoming
    I've been blessed to learn from you
                    and your teachers–
                    present in all that you do
                    anew with the actions of now
                    young women

on the move for justice
speaking truths loudly
hearts proudly alight with fires
lit by Ancestors fighting for rights
your embers still warms us now

and like them
when you're gone
we'll carry your song

and we promise
with your old ways
magic
to always sing along.

KERRI SHYING

emotional laundress

        we
almost lost   you
you almost   lost me

I have packed Kristeva into my wounds
and stitched them
    shut with hair dyed every colour
        of the rainbow
smuggling the canons
    singing Randwick Bells
        eating the little
oyster mushrooms that peeked out
between the half healed
flesh   writing over the strong white scars
    that slow me down
for years   a trench of memory
see all the hammer sees
are nails

my inscription for my   tombstone
is done
no money   own teeth
still accurate

avid to go on
broadcast vegan warning
    the bardo is bloody and
heteronormative
    complain before you leave home
    because i'm not stopping for you

i)

Danny   is the thread   sashiko-sewn
        through all
my lounge-rooms bastes together scraps of
men   pets music poems
we listen
    to Laurie Anderson   every
ten years
surprised
at our longevity
        at contentment
a puddle of gasoline and a match
we fight seasonally
    cats in a bag

this
          the braille topography
                    of a friendship between
                furious outsiders   sharp-witted
                      bent on understanding
we
              mine   ourselves
                like Christmas hampers
                  unpacking
                    just to find the bottom

it turned out
failure to recognise stop signs
     was genius

for the alternate route
                   we should display ourselves
       in a window   with studded cloves
   like hams

    we've   settled   into ground
              below the event horizon of expecting to
   get better
              the near misses

in the realm of the formless
all are welcome
            in deracinated silence without gender
                                 my identity
                              is participatory
                    see me

                                i am
                                 a
                              decorative   and

                meaningless
                      luxury
                  of   zero nourishment

hooked for life on refusal   i release
                                    myself
                                   do the
                                   laundry   play

                              i say
                              be my nothing
                              it's
                              not a kiss to build a dream
                                    on

ii)
hadn't i better   you'll experience true
                  wander   in oblivion   surround   sound
                                                                matte black   from all directions
              angry at my senses   hungry ghosts fly   at us
     i feel around   for where i end   this has become a home
       where the world begins   away   from home
         with eyes tight shut   i float   refusal   my true north
         a tight torso   in thin air   replies   death is frightening

what remains is   the dhamma   in the realm of the formless there are
of no self   only soloists on stage
a comfortable cardigan   permission
and refusal   when you have come this far you have failed
                                                 to recognize several off ramps
the next 8 days i wander in the bardo
                                                              i barely have time   i have
the realm of the formless   forever
black on black
glistens   to decide

the din is every garbage day   tin bins   i notice
                                                 a familiar shape

                    angry men

that noise
    clacking   shooting
        gibbering
like a pinball machine in motion
    itches   bones
    mescaline made from
        the universe
is hard to stomach   but if you keep it
                                    down
for 20 mins

i'm
as empty and alone
as light

warm inside the cardigan
knowing my home
my   boneless exclamation
Danny   this looks easy
hear you
i agree

BETH SPENCER

Dress me up

In the nether region of the wardrobe my mother's silver wedding shoes
are a beacon in that long hallway where the bedrooms hide like bodies.

In the pink of a bathroom Sunday she gives a quick sponge before church
— underarms and privates, skin holy in the glow from dimpled glass.

The secret parts of her. The softest flesh.
The smell of soap and shame and sweat.

She fastens the clip of the blue diamante necklace. The promise
of peace in war, iced now into tears of feeding and dishes, the long

capture of children's bodies.
And the weddings (white veil, chink in the armour).

Outside, tall sons stride long legs in gumboots.
Inside, I parade hobbled high in silver dreams.

Past uncle-art on the walls, driftwood sculptures, across green
carpet like paddocks where the cows low in grief, their milk

a shaft of light in a cup under the chaff motes.
And the sad soft chewing of it all, and the click of silver.

ZAINAB Z SYED

A love like that

When there is a war raging outside
and they give me a stage
I take up the rosary:

Rabbi-shrahli sadri. Wa yassirli amri. Wa-hlul ‘uqdatamin lisani. Yafqahu qawli
$$\text{(Quran, 20:25-28)}$$

O, you gentle creations of God
may every word you utter be the most beautiful sunset I have ever seen
may you find refuge
from hearts that are not humble
tongues that are not wise
eyes that have forgotten how to cry
and palms that do not know the weight of love

love burns slowly

there are often decades that pass between prayers made
and prayers answered
so hurl every sweet nothing into this storm, and
watch it downpour as redemption.

My ancestors did not cross the border
for me to carry shards in my chest
these incisions are meant to let the light in
so let the light in

let the earth testify that you never put her children into graves
say to the angels: *Yes!*
We are capable of such wretchedness
but we chose to plant forgiveness
we were not colonized by the un-truth
we did not make museums of our faith
we were *muhsin*;
leaving everything more beautiful than we first found it.

Come! Search for the Truth with me
in the nightingale's song

and the breath of the wild horse at dawn
the way rocks skip and rainforests breathe
I want to apprentice myself to the way He has written you so beautiful.

On most days I choose silence
because speech is divine and
Lord, I am a sinner

See, every rustle is scripture
and we will probably catch fire
but the sun finds high noon only after setting
so be shipwreck
if it means they will believe in ocean
be chimes
if they will believe in wind
be burnt at the stake and watch it become garden like Abraham
if they will believe in a love like that

What is a love like that?

It looks something like forty years from now,
Gabriel descends to the cave
and finds you in the audience of One

and you, with your arms wide open
a rose that gave fragrance to every hand that crushed it
will soar!

So when they give you a stage and there is a war raging outside
say
*"O my Lord, expand for me my breast, and ease for me my task and untie the knot
from my tongue that they may understand my speech"*   (Quran, 20:25-28)

and then watch, what happens to a love like that!

ANNE WALSH

The Wolves of Mayo *(for my grandmother)*

You kept Irish on your tongue like the last Christmas candy
you try to keep going because you can't get any more like that
you were never a local anywhere I ever saw you not since you left
Ireland so long before that your memory of it slanted like snow
under someone else's memory of a streetlamp in winter
      That furious quiet that anchorite white
            an electric pink prayer falling up from its face
And you never went back
I'm sure that's why I was born with a chest that's a ship of goodbye
why I've left every place I've ever lived, why *I'm* a local nowhere
Why I carry goodbye with me like a business card, like hello
Why no one can place the where of how I speak
because the where of what's underneath my voice
isn't from here, it's from elsewhere, the between worlds
      I write past midnight, that the roots of Alder's bridge
         Me The *Elsewherefarer*
since all my people before me were pulled from the trees
who cradled us in swaddling leaves and in rain that meant Everything
would be well and our wells deep as our own divining
the sticks didn't matter, we were walking aquifers
we didn't have to look for water, it was us, the song
      Of stars in blanket bog and the sweet scent of turf
         fire thick as chocolate in moonlit rooms
After blown out candles and clayed slanes' wings rested by the flames,
it was no Big Bang to hold a stick that would turn for us
It was just to hold the Hazel, the hand of a lover
not to lead us to water, we were horse and felt where it was
The land we knew was a little bit of mud mixed with ocean my dreams
are still of dark seas like the mad core off Inishmore
where at night there's no horizon only a crow wing portal
between here
      and Tír
          na nÓg
We didn't come back in the morning

but we return every night by moonlight in my Clipper heart you
were nineteen when you had to leave Breaffy
and your dad's new grave and the dog by the door,
twenty-one when you married a man in Philadelphia who hit you
when he drank and he drank all the time, how the time must've dragged
      A dead limb,
              a possum shocked by cat's teeth
A fox the colour of sunset gutted by a man in a coat
who blew a horn before he hit you made a sport of it
But there's shale colour in a fox tale, ochre seams, the geology of listening
to stars biting into the sky of your eyelids
in the cathedral made of trees god built when she first fell
      in love was your language
             not the tick of a clock with only a big hand
sounding eternity in its hour of silence, set to the cuckoo bruises on your arm
and to the endlessnesses of you and the kids hiding
in the closet, untimeable forevers
(my hour ghost limbs still feel safer in a closet)
You couldn't save them from him, especially poor little Joe
Did you dream then of the wolves of Mayo?
      An even older memory than yours, could you hear
             them howling in Philadelphia so far past
real midnight that Primary Night was again
and you ran in it with the wolves
and they spoke Irish
and the night sounded like a river
Did you remember then?
      Did you remember the language of yourself in All
            that blue light and lips curled off fangs
Running from a man to the wolves?
Tell me in Irish our Christmas candy language,
light my fairy tongue with choice
It seems I've made all the wrong ones, like you trusted
false loves who don't speak tree

    Now fifty
           sleeping on a friend's couch
Forge in my smithy mouth your master silver work of loss
And I will speak in our leaf language, with our alphabet of trees
and play with little Joe in all the Birches, Rowans, Alders,
Willows, Ash, Hawthorns, Oaks, Holly, Hazel, Apple, Vine
Ivy, Reed, Blackthorn, Elder, Fir, Gorse, Heather, Poplar, Yew and Pine
      Who taught us Irish, that ear singing
           their lullaby of wind
Of rain, of wolves, of worlds, of no goodbyes

JEN WEBB
Refuse/refuge

Refuse/refuge

The verandah tipped to the north and she went over too and lay on the sweet timbers staring into the eye of the world, which she later realised was no more than the shining moon, at the edge of the neighbours' roof. And in fact the verandah had not tipped, she later agreed, in therapy, but she had; or had been tipped, said the counsellor, though the passive voice distressed her. Not that it matters from this distance, time having done its tricksy thing and cantered away before returning like a curious horse to check out the mess it left behind. She reaches out a hand and clasps the ropes that are draped across the sky, hauls herself to her feet, begins again.

From the family album #2

It's evening, and the sun has left a watercolour wash across the sky, and birds are flying into its light, heading nestward. We have poured the second wine of the evening and placed our Uber order of pho for two. You are distressed about folk in distant nations, slaughtered by soldiers or lacking water or watching the glaciers fade. The child is distressed because his cracker has shattered on the kitchen floor. I cannot determine what should or should not be, but still I can comfort a child. As I start to ask your help, you turn from the window and look at me, something unreadable in your gaze.

ALI WHITELOCK
LOOK AT HER

(after Lucian Freud's painting, 'And the Bridegroom')

AT THE GALLERY, i ask my friend what she thinks the painting's about. she says it looks like they just had sex. i say, 'are you crazy? it looks like they've been married for thirty years, there's no fucking way they're still having sex! look at her,' i go on, 'she's exhausted. look at her hair, dangling off the end of the mattress trying to escape from her head. look at her eyes, closed to what she cannot change, accepting what she cannot see. and look at him,' i demand, 'legs splayed, the weight of his knee pushing her to the brink where she clings on for reasons even she can't quite understand.' And it's not that they're exactly unhappy together. lonely, perhaps. resigned—not even the shared heart shock following the death of their pet dog strong enough to araldite them together. 'and another thing,' i press on, 'look at the disgrace of the blanket they're lying on--like a thick linen tablecloth that needs ironing.' More than once i've stood in front of that painting, imagined taking two corners of the blanket & yanking it as though from under a perfectly set dinner table—flashy wine glasses, silver plated salt shakers, ostentatious gravy boats & pompous twelve inch dinner plates go flying. she goes flying too. lands on the bare floorboards, her eyes closed still. he lands on top of her, crushing her like he always does.

ALISON WHITTAKER
optimal

On the treadmill
everything dissolves.

I pop the network of veins
on my calf from the effort of

heaving my lardy murru up
the varying six to ten incline

I am advised to do this for
maybe an hour and eat
eighteen hundred calories (max) a day

I am minimising my health risks
inherent apparently
as an Aboriginal woman

from a long line of big yinarr
who I guess died excruciatingly and

humiliatingly and early and in public
like I am now seven hours a week not
because of a colony or anything but
because they ate and lived
sub-optimally as colonial subjects.

So I'm optimising.

On the treadmill I find it hard to breathe,
or talk, so
sorry this poem is so stilted or

my legs tremble in my pursuit of the gap
between them and the gap between us.

All I can think about,
aside from my pending mortality,

is even more imminently shitting myself,
when I eventually do it's like black tar.

I puke all over
myself often,
unrelated to the treadmill.
I go to see a dietician.
I tell her about the vomiting
when I submit a diet plan.
She says 'bulimics
usually know a bit more
about nutrition.'
She says 'see, rice crackers.'
Disappointing because
I ate them optimally.
Flavourless, portion-controlled.

A row is a hundred of them
calorie things (max).
She suggests keto.

On the way home I go
by Sumo Salad, right? And a
woman takes my picture —
a visual metaphor, probably. Fatties
aren't
meant to show that we know that.
Or
that we know that they know that
we know.

Anyway, I do that (keto and speed)
until my liver pops out in weird x-ray
spots and all the weight I lost turns me

yellow so they pull out my gallbladder
it was 'hmm, very bad' and also my
teeth rot. I am given instructions to not
eat fats or too many carbs. On the way

home I go by my upper-gastro specialist,
the one't took out my gall bladder, his office is
next to a sign about gastric sleeve weight loss
surgery. I'm crying out the front and another
fat girl takes my photo! Does she know that I
know that she knows that I know? Do I know
that she knows? No.

The doctors won't tell me why
they won't give me post-surgery
morphine. When I'm waking up
I hear 'breathing' and
'at her BMI' and 'sat'.

Back at work, I am reading inquest findings.
In them I see fat blak people pinned down
by scores of cops, people like me who just
somehow spontaneously die of heart
failure because, randomly and out of
nowhere, their own big torsos were
'obscuring their airways' when they were
pressed flat into the ground
for optimal control.

When I am arrested, they
take me to a pub bathroom
and make me piss with the door open.

I looked down at my foul and heaving belly,
which in its comorbid and racial risky mass is
covering my cunt and my dignity, and I think
a quiet and optimal 'thank you.'

JESSICA L WILKINSON

Princess Fantasy, according to Jean Baudrillard

I like to be a free spirit.
—*Lady Diana Spencer*

Order of Sacrament

In the beginning, Diana is a child holding: a white
rabbit; a ballet pose; the hand of Mother Teresa.
In the beginning, she is walking down a very long
aisle—the veil is a veil and not yet a perversion of
reality. Lucky Duch, born into privilege, able to faff
around and fail high school. Lady Di in love, left
wanting. Fingers down the throat, downcast.
She is lonely. We note the us-ness of her affairs,
praise the way she grips a cause, gloveless. When
the wreck circulates we hold pictures close to our
noses, squint, attempt to make out bone or blood.

Order of Maleficence

The veil is a curtain and it weighs a tonne. Look:
Lady Di, born into privilege—that old fairytale,
recast. Diana of many collars: pie-crust, sailor,
Peter Pan. Diana hairstyles everywhere and not
quite right. Lick a finger, flip the page on Di, black
dress twirling on the White House floor. We buy
all angles: humanitarian Di, adulterer Di, tiara-
-bedazzled with flash-light choking at the centre
of the throat. *Golly*, she says, and it enters
the narrative. When the story wanders, we follow
suit: a protracted screeching of gears and wheels.

Order of Sorcery

A curtain is drawn on the absence of flesh; running on
a dearth of footage, Diana is raised up and up in a recurring
dream, nostalgia waving like a stiff, royal hand. Human-
itarian Di, Adulterer Di, Flash Di, getting in and out of cars,
stretching out an arm, a hand. Diana legs ("lovely") stride
into Warhol retrograde: Naomi-Watts-Diana; Diana as
portrayed in *The Crown*; So-and-so-actress, Di-cast—lucky
duck in the crosshairs, blushed and ripe, saying *no no no*
behind a tennis racket shield. Diana-trained to overlook
the never-deadness of the fantasy, the trick of her big eyes,
directed sideways: Princess-of-the-People-craving-images.

A Copy of [   ]

Sunk into the vacuum of unloved-ness,
images of sacrifice and escape: a swarm
reaching fever-pitch come seasonal Net-
flix discharge. Signals re-stock Lady Di as
mug or shower curtain, as commemorative
postage stamp embroidered onto fabric fit
for high kitsch vest. Opinions cast on, cast
off. All of our eyes have opened into mouths:
we gulp down pixelated diamond-crusted
fairytales, never satisfied—our colons lined
with Diana découpage, our colons filled up
on empty.

MANAL YOUNUS

you must
carve windows into the doors that your keys won't open

it can be tiring
while you're climbing through makeshift windows and loopholes
leaping from stepping stones
that float on nothingness
while you carry the bruises
from every footprint on your back
every strain on your shoulder blades

know that sometimes
your fight will be against parts of the very body you treasure

so
hold the corners of your lips in place
say few words
but make sure every one reverberates
in the rooms that have been kept from your reach

then,
catch the little bit of breath
that is still yours
that you haven't yet wasted
on justifying you

finally,
though it may never come
keep waiting for the day
that your being
is no longer a protest

SISTA ZAI ZANDA

A Poem In Honour Of A Lioness Perfecting Her Balance Of Inner/Outer Power

Gentleness is her Superpower.
And,
She works it   g e n e r o u s
But
Just like a Lioness.

See:
Overstep or disrespect and
Soon. You. Will. Learn.

  Yes, she is a Lioness.
    She regally balances

Supple Softness   And   Agile Fierceness.

    And this delicate balance of power,
  Well, it's rarely welcomed.
  But
She'll be the first to tell you,
Ever so gently,
"Your Fear is none of my business."

Gentleness.   Gentleness.   Gentleness.   Gentleness.
               Gentleness.

Gentleness is her superpower.
And she works it, g e n e r o u s
But
Like a Lioness
Because she overstands the Mystery:
Her gentleness complements and strengthens
An unapologetic roar and uncompromising defence.
As the ancients say:
Shumba musango haizi yokutamba.

Gentleness is her superpower.
And she works it,
Generous
But
Like a Lioness—
So, overstep or disrespect, then
Soon. You. Will. Learn.
Yes!
She is a Lioness.

BIOGRAPHIES

CONTRIBUTOR BIOGRAPHIES

Jordie Albiston has published twelve poetry collections and a handbook on poetic form. Albiston possesses an ongoing pre-occupation with mathematical constructs and constraints, and the possibilities offered in terms of poetic structure. Her work has won many awards, including the 1996 Mary Gilmore Award, the 2010 NSW Premier's Prize and the 2019 Patrick White Literary Award. She lives in Melbourne.

Ivy Alvarez's poetry collections include *The Everyday English Dictionary*, *Disturbance* (Seren) and *Mortal*. Her latest collection is *Diaspora, Vol. L* (San Mateo: Paloma Press, 2019). Born in the Philippines and raised in Australia, she lived in Wales for almost a decade, before arriving in New Zealand in 2014. ivyalvarez.com.

Cassandra Atherton is an award-winning writer and scholar of prose poetry. She was a Visiting Scholar in English at Harvard University, a Visiting Fellow in Literature at Sophia University, Tokyo and is currently Professor of Writing and Literature at Deakin University. Her most recent books of prose poetry are *Leftovers* (2020) and *Fugitive Letters* (2020). She is currently working on a book of prose poetry on the atomic bomb with funding from the Australia Council. Cassandra co-wrote *Prose Poetry: An Introduction* (2020) and co-edited *The Anthology of Australian Prose Poetry* (2020) with Paul Hetherington.

Tusiata Avia (MNZM) is a multi-award-winning New Zealand poet and children's author whose work explores Pasifika and cross-cultural themes, as well as the borders between traditional and contemporary life, and between place and the self. Avia's poetry show *Wild Dogs Under My Skirt* has toured both nationally and internationally, most recently to New York. Her last two books, *Fale Aiutu – Spirit House* and *The Savage Coloniser Book*, both shortlisted for the Ockham New Zealand Book Awards. She is a creative writing lecturer at the Manukau Institute of Technology.

Maryam Azam is a Pakistani-Australian writer and teacher from Western Sydney. Her debut poetry collection *The Hijab Files* (Giramondo, 2018) was shortlisted for the Anne Elder award and Mary Gilmore award. Maryam welcomed her first child in 2020. Currently she is interested in writing the experience of new motherhood during a pandemic.

Yasaman Bagheri is a 22-year-old writer and a political refugee. In 2013, she fled Iran due to religious and political persecution and sought asylum in Australia. From the age of 15 she was incarcerated in Australia's offshore detention regime for a total of five years, moving between Christmas Island Detention Centre, Darwin Detention Centre, and the Australian-run offshore detention centre on Nauru. In 2018, she was medically evacuated to Australia and is currently living in Queensland. Yasaman is not allowed to study but this hasn't stopped her from writing.

Bidisha is a writer, broadcaster and filmmaker. Her latest non-fiction publications are *The Future of Serious Art*, about how emergent artists' careers might develop in the years to come, and *Asylum and Exile: Hidden Voices*, based on her outreach work in prisons, refugee charities and detention centres. Bidisha writes about the arts, culture and current affairs for the main UK broadsheets and broadcasts for BBC TV and radio, Channel 4 News and Sky News. Her first short film, *An Impossible Poison*, premiered in November 2017 to widespread critical acclaim. Her latest short film series *Aurora* premiered in October 2020.

Merlinda Bobis has had 4 novels, 6 poetry books and a collection of short stories published and 10 dramatic works performed. Her novel *Locust Girl, A Lovesong* received the Christina Stead Prize for Fiction in the NSW Premier's Literary Awards and the Philippine National Book Award. Her poetry collection *Accidents of Composition* was Highly Commended for the ACT Book of the Year Award. Her new book of short stories *The Kindness of Birds* will be launched in May 2021.

Candy Bowers is a radical mischief-maker, poet, playwright and actor born on Wiradjeri land to South African political refugees. Winner of the 2018 Geoffrey Milne- Contribution to Independent Theatre Green Room Association Award, the 2019 Screen Australia/AiF MentorLA Fellowship and 2020 AWGIE nomination for her lyrical theatre work for young audiences, *One the Bear*. Candy has crafted a body of work that offers audiences and readers the vision of an intersectional future in full technicolour.

Jillian Boyd-Bowie is a Torres Strait Islander woman from the Samsep and Zagareb tribes of Erub and Mer. She was born and raised on Thursday Island, Torres Strait. To date, Jillian has published two children's books, Bakir and Bi and its sequel Bid Buai (Dolphin People). Bakir and Bi was a winner at the 2012 Black&write! Fellowship competition and achieved international acclaim when it was chosen for the White Raven's Catalogue produced by the International Youth Library in Germany.

Melinda Bufton is the author of *Girlery* (2014) and *Superette* (2018). Her work has also appeared in numerous publications including *Cordite*, *Southerly* and *Rabbit Poetry Journal*. In 2019 she was the winner of the inaugural Charles Rischbieth Jury Poetry Prize as well as the Helen Anne Bell Poetry Bequest, the latter resulting in the publication of her third collection, *Moxie* (2020).

Michelle Cahill was born in Kenya to Indian parents. She has received prizes in poetry and fiction. Her short story collection *Letter to Pessoa* was awarded the 2017 NSW Premier's Literary Awards for New Writing (Glenda Adams Award) and was shortlisted for the 2017 Steele Rudd Queensland Literary Award. *Visvarupa* was shortlisted in the Victorian Premier's Literary Awards. She has received grants from the Australia Council, the Copyright Agency Limited and an Australian Postgraduate Award. Michelle held the Red Room Poetry Fellowship in 2020. Her novel *Woolf* is forthcoming with Hachette.

Vahni Capildeo FRSL is Writer in Residence at the University of York and Contributing Editor for *PN Review*. Their current non-fiction research focus is on silence. Recent poetry publications are *Skin Can Hold* (Carcanet, 2019), interactive texts for readers to bring to life; *Odyssey Calling* (Sad Press, 2020), a bluegreen book of migrations; *Light Site* (Periplum Poetry, 2020), 'expanded translations' including calypso voicings of sixteenth-century love lyrics, and *The Dusty Angel* (Oystercatcher, 2021), a series of walks, nocturnes and lullabies in real-time and deep-time Port of Spain. Capildeo contributed a series of pandemic memoirs as dispatches to the Poetry on the Move Festival 2020.

Anne Casey is an award-winning Irish poet/writer living in Australia. A journalist, magazine editor, legal author and media communications director for 30 years, she is author of *out of emptied cups* and *where the lost things go*, with a third collection and a chapbook forthcoming in 2021. Anne's work is widely published internationally, ranking in The Irish Times' Most Read. She is a PhD student at the University of Technology Sydney, supported by an Australian Government Research Training Program Scholarship.

Bonny Cassidy is a settler of Irish and German descent living on Dja Dja Wurrung lands. She is the author of four poetry collections, most recently, *Chatelaine* (Giramondo Publishing, 2017) which was shortlisted for the 2018 Prime Minister's Literary Awards. With Jessica L Wilkinson, Bonny co-edited the anthology, *Contemporary Australian Feminist Poetry* (Hunter Publishers, 2016). She teaches Creative Writing at RMIT University, Melbourne, where she is a member of the non/fictionLab research group and the Bundyi Girri project team.

Claire G. Coleman is a Wirlomin-Noongar writer and poet. She either lives in Naarm (Melbourne) or on the road. Her novels *Terra Nullius* (winner of the Norma K Hemming Award) and *The Old Lie* are published in Australia by Hachette and in North America by Small Beer Press, and her non-fiction book *Lies, Damned Lies* is out in September 2021 from Ultimo Press. She is also on the cultural advisory committee for Agency, a Not-for-profit Indigenous arts Consultancy.

Emilie Collyer lives on unceded Wurundjeri land, where she writes poetry, plays and prose. Her writing has appeared most recently in *Rabbit*, *Australian Poetry Journal*, *Witness Performance* and *Cordite*. She received a 2020 Varuna Publisher Introduction Fellowship with Giramondo Publishing. Award-winning and nominated plays include *Super Perfect*, *Contest*, *Dream Home* and *The Good Girl* which has had multiple international productions. She is currently a PhD candidate in creative writing at RMIT.

H I Cosar is a Sydney based teacher, bilingual poet and community artist who is interested in writing for the page as well as stage. Her first collection of poems, *Hijabi in Jeans* was published in 2018 by Guillotine Press. Her work has been published in the anthologies *Kaleidoscope*, *Poetry without Borders*, *On Second Thought*, *Can I Tell You a Secret* as well as in *Mascara Literary Review* and the *Australian Poetry Journal*. She likes working on projects of intersectionality in particular those platforms where poetry meets other art forms. She has performed as a feature in reading circles, 'Live Poets Society', 'Gugubarra' as well as experimental theatre, 'The Prophet - Remix' and 'Night Sky'.

Judith Nangala Crispin is an artist and poet of Bpangerang descent. She spends part of every year living and working in the Tanami Desert, in Warlpiri Country, where she maintains strong community links. Her work deals with issues of displacement and connection to Country. Judith has published two collections of poetry, *The Myrrh-Bearers* (Puncher & Wattmann, 2015), and *The Lumen Seed* (Daylight Books, 2017). Her illustrated verse novel, *The Dingo's Noctuary*, will be published in late 2021.

Tricia Dearborn is an award-winning queer poet, writer and editor based in Sydney. Her latest poetry collection is *Autobiochemistry* (UWAP, 2019). Her work has been widely published in literary journals, and featured in anthologies including *The Anthology of Australian Prose Poetry* (2020) and *Contemporary Australian Poetry* (2016). She was a judge of the 2019 University of Canberra Vice-Chancellor's International Poetry Prize, and guest poetry editor for *Rabbit: a journal for non-fiction poetry 31: The Science Issue* (2020). Tricia also writes fiction: 'The Case of G: A Child Raised by Trains' won the 2020 Neilma Sidney Short Story Prize.

Winnie Dunn is a writer of Tongan descent from Mount Druitt. She is the General Manager of Sweatshop Literacy Movement and holds a Bachelor of Arts from Western Sydney University. Winnie's work has been published in the *Sydney Review of Books*, *The Saturday Paper*, *Griffith Review*, *Meanjin*, *SBS Voices*, *The Guardian*, *Huffington Post*, *Southerly* and *Cordite*. She is the editor of several critically acclaimed anthologies, most notably *Sweatshop Women*, which is Australia's first and only publication produced entirely by women of colour. Winnie is currently working on her debut novel as the recipient of a CAL Ignite grant.

Zoe Dzunko is a poet, editor and Lecturer at RMIT University. Her work has appeared in numerous Australian and international publications including *The Age*, *Australian Book Review*, *Southerly*, *Guernica*, *Tin House*, *The Fanzine*, *Prelude* et al. and received support from the Bread Loaf Writers' Conference, Tin House Writer's Workshop, and Yale Writers' Conference. She is the author of *Selfless* (TAR).

Caren Florance is a queer typo-bibliographic artist, writer and designer who currently lives and works on Ngunnawal country. *Lost in Case*, a book of coded feminist concrete poetry derived from letterpress practice, was published by Cordite Books in 2019 and was shortlisted for the Mary Gilmore Award for Poetry. https://carenflorance.com

Eugenia Flynn is a writer, arts worker and community organiser. As an Aboriginal (Larrakia and Tiwi), Chinese Malaysian and Muslim woman, Eugenia works within her multiple communities to create change through literature, art, politics and community engagement. Eugenia's thoughts on the politics of race, gender and culture have been published widely. Her essays, articles and short stories have been published in *IndigenousX*, *NITV*, the *Guardian Australia*, *Peril magazine* and the anthology *#MeToo: Stories From the Australian Movement*.

Es Foong is an emerging poet, flash fiction writer and spoken word performer living in Naarm (Melbourne). Their poetry has been included in *Australian Poetry Journal*, *Cold Mountain Review* and *Audacious 4*, Melbourne Spoken Word's audio journal. On-stage, they are the poetic analogue of heavy-metal karaoke. Off-stage, they eat identity labels for breakfast. They live online at waffleirongirl.com.

Zenobia Frost (@zenfrost) is a poet from Brisbane whose latest collection, *After the Demolition* (Cordite Books), explores grief, queer joy, place attachment and belonging. She won the 2020 Wesley Michel Wright Award and Queensland Premier's Young Publishers and Writers Award, and has performed across Australia. In 2020, Zenobia edited coffee-table history book *Art Starts Here: 40 Years of Metro Arts*.

Kween G is both an industry and cultural leader and emerging Afro-Australian Icon. Renowned for provocative, unflinching and authentic Hip Hop content, Kween G delivers a dynamic style as an MC, performer and Hip Hop artist. Kween G is often described as 'consciousness-raising'. Her fighting spirit – for women's rights and those in disadvantaged communities – courage and humility have earned her respect across the country. Kween G has been, and continues to develop as a powerful advocate for social Justice awareness through the arts and is consistent in her care and commitment to her music.

Mindy Gill is the recipient of the Queensland Premier's Young Writers and Publishers Award and the Australian Poetry/NAHR Eco-Poetry Fellowship in Val Taleggio, Italy. Her poetry and criticism have appeared in *Award Winning Australian Writing*, the Institute of Modern Art, the Queensland Art Gallery, *Sydney Review of Books* and *Australian Book Review*.

Elena Gomez is a poet and book editor living in Melbourne. She is the author of *Admit the Joyous Passion of Revolt* (2020), *Body of Work* (2018) and several chapbooks. Her poems and essays have been published widely in print and online.

Charmaine Papertalk Green is an award-winning poet from Midwest Western Australia and a member of the Wajarri, Badimaya and Nhanagardi Wilunyu cultural groups of the Yamaji Nation. Her publications include *Just Like That* (Fremantle Art Press, 2007); *Tiptoeing Tod the Tracker* (Oxford University Press, 2014); collaboration with WA poet John Kinsella, *False Claims of Colonial Thieves* (Magabala Books, 2018); *Nganajungu Yagu* (Cordite Publishing Inc, 2019); and numerous anthologies and other publications. She lives in Geraldton WA.

Eloise Grills is an award-winning comics artist, essayist, critic and poet living in Daylesford, on Dja Dja Wurrung country. Her first collection of poetry, *If you're sexy and you know it slap your hams* (Subbed In), was shortlisted for the Mary Gilmore Award. She is currently working on her first collection of illustrated essays, *big beautiful female theory*, to be published by Affirm Press in early 2022.

Susan Hawthorne is the author of nine collections of poetry and a verse novel. Her collection *Cow* (2011) was shortlisted for the Kenneth Slessor Poetry Prize in the NSW Premier's Literary Awards and was a Finalist in the Audre Lorde Lesbian Poetry prize (USA). *Earth's Breath* (2009) was shortlisted for the Judith Wright Poetry Prize. Her most recent collections are *Lupa and Lamb* (2014) and *The Sacking of the Muses* (2019).

Sarah Holland-Batt is an award-winning poet, editor and critic, and an Associate Professor within the Creative Industries Faculty at QUT. Her most recent book, *The Hazards* (UQP, 2015), won the Prime Minister's Literary Award for Poetry. She is presently Chair of *Australian Book Review*, and *The Australian*'s poetry columnist.

LK Holt lives in Narrm/Melbourne. She is the recipient of a NSW Premiers' Literary Award and the Grace Leven Prize for Poetry, and has been longlisted for the ALS Gold Medal. Her latest poetry collection, *Birth Plan*, was shortlisted in the 2020 Victorian Premiers' Literary Awards and the 2020 Prime Ministers' Literary Awards.

Zeina Issa is a Sydney based Australian Lebanese poet, translator and published columnist. Her work has appeared in *Australian Poetry*, *Mascara*, *Red Room Poetry* and *Contrappasso*, and has also been anthologised.

Eleanor Jackson is a Filipino Australian poet, performer and arts producer. She is the author of *Gravidity and Parity* (Vagabond Press) and *A Leaving* (Vagabond Press); her live album, *One Night Wonders*, is produced by Going Down Swinging. She is the producer of the Melbourne Poetry Map and a former Editor in Chief of *Peril Magazine*, Board Member of Queensland Poetry Festival and Vice-Chair of the Stella Prize. She is currently Chair of *Peril Magazine*.

Lizzie Jarrett is a sovereign woman from the Gumbaynggirr, Bundjalung, Dunghutti clans and is a direct descendant of the original Stolen Generations. Lizzie is a First Nations advocate/activist assisting with a high volume of casework involving First Nations people who have suffered discrimination and violence at the hands of government agencies or others and are seeking legal remedy. She makes it her life duty to help advocate for her peoples' rights through activism, poetry, art, music and volunteering to the community.

Jill Jones' most recent books include *Wild Curious Air*, *A History Of What I'll Become* and *Viva the Real*, which was shortlisted for the 2019 Prime Minister's Literary Awards for Poetry and the 2020 John Bray Award. In 2015 she won the Victorian Premier's Prize for Poetry for *The Beautiful Anxiety*. Her work is represented in a number of major anthologies including *The Macquarie PEN Anthology of Australian Literature*, *Contemporary Australian Poetry*, and *The Penguin Anthology of Australian Poetry*.

Gabrielle Journey Jones (Gabe) lives on Yuin Country, Far South Coast NSW. She shares Maori and African bloodlines and has performed her poetry at local, national and international events for over 20 years. Gabe is inspired by creative communities which celebrate diversity, artivism and inclusion. Gabe's first collection of poetry *Spoken Medicine* (2017) was released by Ginninderra Press. They are in the process of publishing her second anthology *Etymology of Courage* (2021). Contact Gabe at www.poeticpercussion.com.au

Jeanine Leane is a Wiradjuri writer, poet and academic from southwest New South Wales. Her poetry and short stories have been published in *Hecate*, *The Journal for the Association of European Studies of Australia*, *Australian Poetry Journal*, *Antipodes*, *Overland*, *Westerly* and the *Australian Book Review*. Jeanine has published widely in the area of Aboriginal literature, writing otherness and creative non-fiction. In 2019 she was the recipient of the Red Room Poetry Fellowship. In 2020 Jeanine edited *Guwayu – for all times* – a collection of First Nations Poetry commissioned by Red Room Poetry and published by Magabala Books.

Carissa Lee is a Noongar woman born on Wemba-Wemba country. She is currently undertaking her PhD on First Nations theatre through the University of Melbourne. Although Carissa is predominantly an academic writer, she has been writing poetry and short stories since she was little. Carissa's writing has featured in publications *Witness Performance*, *Book Riot*, *Red Room Poetry*, *ArtsHub*, *IndigenousX* and *Junkee*.

Kate Lilley is a widely-published queer, feminist poet-scholar based in Sydney. Her first book, *Versary* (Salt 2002), won the Grace Leven Prize. Her second, *Ladylike* (UWAP 2012), was shortlisted for the NSW Premier's Prize. Her most recent book, *Tilt* (Vagabond 2018) won the Victorian Premier's Award for Poetry in 2019. She is the editor of *Dorothy Hewett: Selected Poems* (UWAP 2010) and *Margaret Cavendish: The Blazing World and other writings* (Penguin Classics).

Bronwyn Lovell is an Adelaide-based writer. Her poetry has featured in *Best Australian Poems*, *Meanjin*, *Southerly*, *Australian Poetry*, *Cordite*, *Antipodes*, *Strange Horizons* and more. She has won the Val Vallis Award and been shortlisted for the Judith Wright, Fair Australia, Newcastle, Bridport, and Montreal prizes. Her essays have been published by the journal of *Science Fiction Film and Television*, *The Conversation* and the *National Gallery of Victoria*. She teaches creative writing and screen studies at the University of South Australia.

Melissa Lucashenko is a multi-award winning Bundjalung novelist from Brisbane. She is a Walkley Award winner for her non-fiction writing and a founding member of human rights group Sisters Inside.

Jennifer Maiden has published 34 books: 26 poetry collections, 6 novels and 2 nonfiction works. Her awards include 3 Kenneth Slessor and 2 C.J. Dennis Prizes, the Victorian Prize for Literature, the Christopher Brennan Award, 2 Age Poetry Book of Year Awards, The Age Book of the Year as such, and the ALS Gold Medal. Latest books from Quemar Press: Poetry: *Biological Necessity*; *The Espionage Act*; *brookings: the noun*; *Selected Poems 1967-2018*; *Appalachian Fall*; Novels: *Play With Knives 1&2, 3&4, 5*; Non-fiction: *Workbook Questions*; *The Cuckold and the Vampires*.

Selina Tusitala Marsh (ONZM, FRSNZ) is the former New Zealand Poet Laureate and has performed poetry for primary schoolers and presidents (Obama), queers and Queens (HRH Elizabeth II). She has published three critically acclaimed collections of poetry, *Fast Talking PI* (2009), *Dark Sparring* (2013), *Tightrope* (2017) and an award-winning graphic memoir, *Mophead* (Auckland University Press, 2019). *Mophead TU: The Queen's Poem* is out now. Selina lectures in Creative Writing and Pacific Literature at the University of Auckland and specialises in critically hearing silenced or marginalised indigenous poetic voices.

Jennifer Kemarre Martiniello is an award winning multidisciplinary artist of Aboriginal (Arrernte), Chinese and Anglo-Celtic descent. She founded the ACT Indigenous Writers Group in 1999. Her awards include the 2000 Canberra Critics Circle Award for Literature, Banjo Paterson Poetry Prize and Henry Lawson Short Story Prize. She is published in national and international journals and anthologies including the Macquarie PEN Anthology of Australian Literature. She has judged the NSW and Queensland Premier's Literary Awards, including the David Unaipon Award for Indigenous Literature.

So Mayer is a writer, bookseller, film curator and organiser. They are the author, most recently, of the essay *A Nazi Word for a Nazi Thing* (Peninsula, 2020), the poetry chapbook *jacked a kaddish* (Litmus, 2018) and poetry collection (O) (Arc, 2015). So works with queer feminist film curation collective Club des Femmes, and campaign and community organisation Raising Films. @Such_Mayer.

Teena McCarthy is a visual artist and poet who works predominantly in painting, photography and performance art. She graduated in 2014 from UNSW Art & Design with a Bachelor of Fine Arts with Distinction. McCarthy is an Italian/Barkindji woman who is a descendant of The Stolen Generations. Her work documents her family's displacement and Aboriginal Australians' loss of Culture and their 'hidden' history. While acknowledging the intergenerational pain of postcolonialism, McCarthy uses wit, humour and pathos to explore her own identity. Synchronicity also comes into play in McCarthy's experimental painting, often determining its outcome and informing its own materiality.

Jazz Money is a Wiradjuri poet and artist currently based on sovereign Gadigal land in Sydney. Her poetry has been widely published nationally and internationally, and reimagined as murals, installations, digital interventions and film. In 2020 Jazz was awarded the David Unaipon Award from the State Library of Queensland and the Australia Council for the Arts First Nations Emerging Career Award. Her debut collection *how to make a basket* from the University of Queensland Press will be released in 2021.

Lorna Munro, or 'Yilinhi', is a Wiradjuri and Gamilaroi woman, multidisciplinary artist and regular radio and podcast host at Sydney's 'Radio Skid Row'. Lorna continues to work tirelessly mastering many art forms, raising funds, supporting and advocating for her Redfern/Waterloo community and her people on the local, national and international stage. She is a 2019 recipient of the Wheeler Centre's Next Chapter writers' scheme.

Dianty Ningrum was born and raised in Indonesia. She recently won second place at the Oxford Brookes International Poetry Competition and was shortlisted for the Montreal International Poetry Competition. Her poems have appeared in *The Scores* and the *Australian Poetry Anthology*. She currently resides in the unceded land of Wurundjeri people of the Kulin Nation.

Maureen Jipyiliya Nampijinpa O'Keefe is a Kaytetye-Walpiri woman born and raised in Ali-Curung. Her family comes from the Devils' Marbles region also known as Karlu Karlu south of Tennant Creek. An acclaimed poet, writer, storyteller, artist and storykeeper, Maureen currently lives in Alice Springs where she continues to write and facilitate writing workshops.

Suneeta Peres da Costa is based in Sydney, on Gadigal land. Her latest book *Saudade* (Giramondo & Transit Books), concerns Portuguese colonial legacies and the Goan diaspora in pre-Independence Angola. It was shortlisted for the 2019 Australian Prime Minister's Literary Awards, the 2020 Adelaide Festival of Literature Awards and a finalist in the 2020 Tournament of Books (USA). A former Fulbright Scholar, Suneeta's literary honours include the Australia Council BR Whiting Residency, Rome, and an Asialink Arts Creative Exchange to North India.

Reneé Pettitt-Schipp's work with asylum seekers in detention on Christmas Island and the Cocos (Keeling) Islands inspired her first collection of poetry, *The Sky Runs Right Through Us*. This collection was shortlisted for the Dorothy Hewett manuscript prize as well as the 2019 CHASS Australia Student Prize. In 2019, *The Sky Runs Right Through Us* also won the Greg Crombie 'Work of the Year' in the Humanities Research Awards, as well as winning the WA Premier's Literary Award for an Emerging Writer. Reneé now lives in WA's Great Southern.

Anupama Pilbrow is the Editor-in-Chief of *The Suburban Review*. She studied mathematics at The University of Melbourne. Her chapbook *Body Poems* was published in 2018 as part of Vagabond Press' deciBels 3 series and she is currently working on a collection of poems about the sense of smell. Her work often deals with diaspora, dialogue, exchange, and gross body stuff.

Felicity Plunkett is the author of *A Kinder Sea* (UQP), *Vanishing Point* (UQP) and the chapbook *Seastrands* (Vagabond), which was published in Vagabond Press' Rare Objects series. She edited *Thirty Australian Poets* (UQP, 2011).

Dr Anne Poelina is a Nyikina Warrwa (Indigenous Australian) woman in the Kimberley region of Western Australia. Poelina is an active Indigenous community leader, human and earth rights advocate, filmmaker and a respected academic researcher. Laureate from the Women's World Summit Foundation (Geneva), Chair of the Martuwarra Fitzroy River Council (www.martuwarrafitzroyriver.org), Adjunct Professor and Senior Research Fellow with Notre Dame University. Poelina is a Visiting Fellow with the Crawford School of Public Policy at the Australian National University, Canberra Australia Water Justice Hub. ORCID: https://orcid.org/0000-0001-6461-7681

Mel Ree trained as an actor, identifies as a messenger, poet and fierce woman. Born in Papua New Guinea to the daughter of a chief, her ancestors sit at the base of her spine spurring her on to tell her story, hoping to spark wildfires within listeners that burn down differences, uniting us in our pain and understanding of this human condition.

Negar Rezvani is a young Iranian poet and refugee. In 2013, she sought asylum in Australia. Negar was forced to live in an offshore processing prison in the middle of the Pacific Ocean for over six years. She lived in Australia on a community detention visa for a further two years before being resettled in the USA. Her first interview was published in *The Guardian* while she was still detained. Her first poem 'My dear prison officer' was featured by Red Room Poetry, and has also appeared in the *Auawirleben* international theatre festival in Bern, Switzerland, and in *KBS* cultural magazine in Germany.

Lynette Riley is a Wiradjuri & Gamilaroi woman from Dubbo and Moree; is an Associate Professor in the Sydney School of Education & Social Work, The University of Sydney; and Program Director for Indigenous Studies and Aboriginal Education. Lynette trained as an infants/primary teacher. She has been a classroom teacher; an Aboriginal Education consultant; worked in TAFE; as State Manager for Aboriginal Education; and as an academic. Her career focus is improving educational delivery for Aboriginal students. Her PhD was conferred in 2017.

Samah Sabawi wages beautiful resistance through art. A recipient of multiple awards, her theatre credits include the critically acclaimed plays *Tales of a City by the Sea* and *THEM*. Sabawi also co-edited *Double Exposure: Plays of the Jewish and Palestinian Diasporas*, winner of the Patrick O'Neill award and co-authored I Remember My Name: Poetry by Samah Sabawi, Ramzy Baroud and Jehan Bseiso, edited by Dr. Vacy Vlazna, winner of the Palestine Book Award.

Sara M. Saleh is a daughter of migrants from Palestine, Egypt, and Lebanon, living and learning on Gadigal land. A long-time human rights campaigner, writer and poet, Sara's essays, poems, and short stories have been published in English and Arabic in *The Guardian*, *SBS*, *Meanjin*, *Australian Poetry Journal*, *Cordite Poetry Review*, and anthologised nationally and internationally. Sara is the first Australian poet to win both the Australian Book Review's 2021 Peter Porter Poetry Prize and the Overland Judith Wright Poetry Prize 2020. Sara co-curated anthology *Arab-Australian-Other: Stories on Race and Identity* (Picador 2019) and is currently developing her debut fiction novel.

Kirli Saunders is a proud Gunai Woman and award-winning international writer of poetry, plays and picture books. She is a teacher, cultural consultant and artist. Her Books include *The Incredible Freedom Machines*, *Kindred* and *Bindi*. Kirli has 8 forthcoming titles with Magabala, Scholastic and Hardie Grant Egmont and is working with Playwriting Australia and Australia Council for the Arts to deliver plays and visual poetry projects. In 2020, Kirli was named the NSW Aboriginal Woman of the Year.

Kerri Shying is the author of four poetry collections, most recently *Knitting Mangrove Roots* (Flying Islands Press, 2019) and *Know Your Country* (Puncher and Wattman, 2020). She is of Wiradjuri and Chinese family, and is also a visual and fibre artist and a respected disability advocate.

Beth Spencer is an award-winning author of poetry and fiction. Her work has frequently been broadcast on ABC-Radio National, and her books include *How to Conceive of a Girl*, *The Party of Life* and *Vagabondage*. In 2018 she won the Carmel Bird Digital Literary Award for the story collection *The Age of Fibs*, which is due out in expanded form as a print book later this year. www.bethspencer.com

Zainab Z. Syed is a Pakistani-Australian writer. Since graduating from Brown University, USA in 2014, she has toured across the world as a performance poet and facilitated art therapy workshops for incarcerated women, trauma victims, and migrants and refugees. She is founder of Pakistan Poetry Slam & was a finalist in the Australian National Poetry Slam. Zainab is currently based in Boorloo/Perth where she works as a Producer of Theatre/Dance.

Anne Walsh is a poet and a story writer. She has been shortlisted twice for both the Newcastle Poetry Prize and the ACU Prize for literature. Her work has been widely published in print and online in Australia and in the U.S. Her two poetry collections are *I Love Like a Drunk Does* published by Ginninderra Press in 2009 and *Intact*, published by Flying Islands Books in 2017. Recently, at the invitation of American actor Tituss Burgess, she read her work as part of Carnegie Hall's inaugural live online concert.

Jen Webb is Distinguished Professor of Creative Practice at University of Canberra. The ACT editor of *Australian Book Review*'s States of Poetry anthology, co-editor of the Mandarin/English anthology *Open Windows: Contemporary Australian Poetry*, and the literary journal *Meniscus*, her most recent poetry collections are *Moving Targets* (Recent Work Press 2018), and *Flight Mode* (with Shé Hawke, Recent Work Press 2020).

Ali Whitelock is the author of two poetry collections, *the lactic acid in the calves of your despair* & *and my heart crumples like a coke can*.Her memoir, *poking seaweed with a stick & running away from the smell* was launched to critical acclaim in Australia & the UK. www.aliwhitelock.com

Alison Whittaker is a Gomeroi poet, essayist and legal academic from Gunnedah in northern NSW.

Jessica L. Wilkinson has published three poetic biographies: *Marionette: A Biography of Miss Marion Davies* (2012); *Suite for Percy Grainger* (2014) and *Music Made Visible: A Biography of George Balanchine* (2019), each with Vagabond Press. She is the founder/managing editor of *Rabbit: a journal for nonfiction poetry* and of the offshoot Rabbit Poets Series. She co-edited *Contemporary Australian Feminist Poetry* (Hunter Publishers, 2016) and is an Associate Professor in Creative Writing at RMIT University, Melbourne.

Manal Younus is a storyteller from Eritrea based on Kaurna Country, South Australia who uses writing and performance to create experiences that encourage audiences to join her in asking questions of themselves and the world around them.

Sista Zai Zanda is an Afrofuturistic Storyteller residing as a guest on Kulin Nations in Narrm. You can keep up with her latest work at https://linktr.ee/sistazai.

EDITOR BIOGRAPHIES

Saba Vasefi is a multi-award-winning journalist, academic, documentary filmmaker and poet. Her poems have appeared in a variety of journals including *Transnational Literature, Wasafiri Magazine of International Contemporary Writing* (UK), *Cordite Poetry*, and *Australian Poetry Journal*. In 2020 she was commissioned by Red Room Poetry to write poems in response to work in the Art Gallery of New South Wales.

Saba writes for *The Guardian* and a number of other outlets, teaches at Macquarie University, and has researched her PhD in accented (exilic) feminist cinema. Her documentary films have screened internationally including for the BBC, the UN, and Amnesty International. She has received more than half a dozen awards for her work on refugee and feminist issues, and has served as an advisor and Ambassador for many refugee causes. She was twice a judge for the Sedigheh Dolatabadi Book Prize for the Best Book on Women's Literature and Women's Issues as well as the BR4R Seeking Asylum Poetry Prize.

She organised the 2016 Diaspora Symposium: Refugees and Asylum Seeker Discourse (including its Social Justice Award), and the 2015 Sydney International Women's Poetry and Arts Festival. She has been mentioned with congratulations on the floor of the New South Wales Legislative Council for these activities, and for her ongoing contribution to women's rights and social justice.

Yvette Henry Holt is a multi-award-winning poet, editor, stand-up comedienne, femin_artist of desert photography, national facilitator of literary workshops, and Chairperson of the First Nations Australia Writers Network FNAWN. Yvette proudly heralds from the Yiman, Wakaman, and Bidjara Nations of Queensland. Having lived in the remote central deserts of Australia for more than twelve years where she continues to write, research, and document her photography for online journals, Yvette's works have been published and numerously anthologised in publication and online for more than two decades.

Melinda Smith is a poet, editor, teacher and performer. Her latest book is *Manhandled* (Recent Work Press, 2020). She is the author of seven other poetry books, including the 2014 Prime Minister's Literary Award winner, *Drag down to unlock or place an emergency call*, and her work has been widely anthologised and translated. She co-edited, with Sara Saleh, the *Australian Poetry Anthology Vol. 8*, and is a former poetry editor of *The Canberra Times*. She lives and writes on unceded Ngunnawal Country.

ACKNOWLEDGEMENTS

This project has been supported by:

Macquarie University
Amnesty International
Australian Poetry Journal
Red Room Poetry
Sydwest Multicultural Services
Sydney Women's Fund
Affinity Intercultural Foundation

www.ingramcontent.com/pod-product-compliance
Lightning Source LLC
Chambersburg PA
CBHW022017290426
44109CB00015B/1211